A Sociology of Shame and Blame

Graham Scambler

A Sociology of Shame and Blame

Insiders Versus Outsiders

palgrave
macmillan

Graham Scambler
Emeritus Professor of Sociology
University College London
London, UK

Visiting Professor of Sociology
Surrey University
Guildford, UK

ISBN 978-3-030-23142-2   ISBN 978-3-030-23143-9 (eBook)
https://doi.org/10.1007/978-3-030-23143-9

© The Editor(s) (if applicable) and The Author(s), under exclusive license to Springer Nature Switzerland AG 2020
This work is subject to copyright. All rights are solely and exclusively licensed by the Publisher, whether the whole or part of the material is concerned, specifically the rights of translation, reprinting, reuse of illustrations, recitation, broadcasting, reproduction on microfilms or in any other physical way, and transmission or information storage and retrieval, electronic adaptation, computer software, or by similar or dissimilar methodology now known or hereafter developed.
The use of general descriptive names, registered names, trademarks, service marks, etc. in this publication does not imply, even in the absence of a specific statement, that such names are exempt from the relevant protective laws and regulations and therefore free for general use.
The publisher, the authors and the editors are safe to assume that the advice and information in this book are believed to be true and accurate at the date of publication. Neither the publisher nor the authors or the editors give a warranty, expressed or implied, with respect to the material contained herein or for any errors or omissions that may have been made. The publisher remains neutral with regard to jurisdictional claims in published maps and institutional affiliations.

Cover illustration: © Melisa Hasan

This Palgrave Pivot imprint is published by the registered company Springer Nature Switzerland AG
The registered company address is: Gewerbestrasse 11, 6330 Cham, Switzerland

Contents

1	Introduction	1
2	Theoretical Perspectives on Shame and Blame	15
3	Asymmetric Lifeworld Encounters	29
4	The Neglected Contributions of Middle-Range Social Theory	47
5	The Salience of Macro-Sociology	61
6	Towards a Sociology of Shaming and Blaming	87
7	Conclusion	105
	References	109
	Index	115

LIST OF TABLES

Table 1.1	Disability in the UK: some statistics	7
Table 2.1	Lifeworld and system	25
Table 2.2	Notions of stigma and deviance	26
Table 3.1	Relations between system and lifeworld from a system perspective	31
Table 3.2	Contexts for sanctioning people and cutting their benefits	38
Table 4.1	Archer's reflexive modalities	49
Table 4.2	A typology of sex work careers, with examples (Scambler, 2007)	50
Table 4.3	Attributes of the transitory autonomous reflexive	55
Table 5.1	The changing class distribution	64
Table 5.2	The capitalist executive	66
Table 5.3	Top 20 facts about refugees and asylum seekers	74
Table 5.4	The dialectic between shame and blame (Scambler, 2018b)	80
Table 5.5	Dark money, dirty politics and think tanks	80
Table 6.1	Jacquet's criteria for effective stigmatisation (Jacquet, 2015)	94

CHAPTER 1

Introduction

Abstract This chapter sets out the major themes of this study of shame and blame. The first describes the relationships between agency, culture and structure. The second emphasises the importance of covering macro-, meso- and micro-perspectives. And the third focuses on the need to consider how change might be accomplished. The four principal reference groups used in the study are then introduced. These are migrants and refugees; the long-term sick and disabled; the homeless; and sex workers. The chapter ends by anticipating the contents of the remaining chapters in the book.

Keywords Shame · Blame · Agency · Culture · Structure · Migration · Sickness/disability · Homelessness · Sex work

It is not possible to identify people as normal, able-bodied, moral, responsible, healthy, law-abiding, insiders, as belonging, and as a host of other positives, unless it is also possible for others in the same society, community or milieu to be seen as abnormal, disabled, immoral, irresponsible, sick, criminal, outsiders or as strangers. Positives are only possible if negatives are too, as Wittgenstein (1958) affirmed in formulating his 'polar opposites argument'. Moreover, these binary distinctions are not without discernible social functions. It was the proto-functionalist Durkheim, anticipating the dominant Parsonian paradigm in America in the 1950s, who noted that recognising, highlighting and sanctioning/punishing the negatives is important, or 'functional', for the continuing stability of social order. Conformance or compliance with the norms that define the social order at any given time and place—that is, that reproduce the status quo—relies on the rooting out of misfits in all their heterogeneity and the variety and severity of the threats they represent.

Social control, as sociologists conventionally term it, can of course be exerted in the absence of overt coercion or repression. For example, in most developed societies it has long been the—unsought and unwanted—function of state-licensed physicians to police the sick to ensure they do not too long resist the capitalist 'imperative to work'. Sanctioning and punishment can take many forms, from executions and imprisonment to barely perceptible strategies of avoidance. The former Labour MP Jack Ashley (1973) recounted his experiences after suddenly and unexpectedly losing his hearing. In the House of Commons dining room soon after he noticed how quickly embarrassed colleagues, even friends, made excuses to slip away, unable, unwilling or simply too impatient to cope with improvised modes of communication. Insiders versus outsiders is a template that allows for an extensive reach, as this volume bears testimony.

So all societies and segments within them, from *actual* regions, localities, communities and neighbourhoods to their less (or almost un-) constrained *virtual* equivalents, have and act out these positive versus negative tensions. Many, if not all, such tensions involve attributions of shame and blame, and these provide the principal focus for this contribution. I shall draw a clear analytic distinction between the two, notwithstanding the tendency in everyday practice, in the 'lifeworld', to use them interchangeably. I shall deploy the term *stigma* to signal episodes of non-conformance. The stigmatised infringe against norms of *shame*. Their infringements do not imply non-compliance or culpability. It is as if they are 'imperfect beings'. The contrast is with *deviance*. Deviance here refers to falling foul of norms of *blame*. Non-compliance is accented. Infringements bring condemnation: deviants are culpable. Whereas shame imputes an 'ontological deficit', deviance reflects a 'moral deficit'.

Three principal themes run through this volume. The first acknowledges the ongoing interplay of agency, culture and structure in the mundane enactments or performance of shame and blame. Agency, I shall contend, is always contextualised by culture and structured (though never structurally determined). Consider the case of a young girl from Myanmar either 'sold' by an impoverished family or trafficked to work in a brothel in Bangkok. The new culture into which she has been inserted is likely suffocating and oppressive to the point of social claustrophobia, yet it would be quite wrong in my view, and insulting, to count her agency as lost: agency can at most be subdued and temporarily misplaced or displaced. Safe sex and the sharing of needles might register low on priorities oriented to day-to-day survival, but neither her reflexivity nor her agency is ever entirely absent. Not even concentration camp confinement and brutality can cancel agency. Agency is part of being human.

Second, a credible sociology of shame and blame must range from and do justice to macro- through meso- to micro-processes. As we shall see, it was Goffman's (1968) signal contribution to illuminate micro-processes via his sensitisation of the concept of stigma (with which mine has some resonance), but he did not extend much beyond brief flirtations with meso-processes. No sociological explanation of the lot of the young girl deposited in the brothel in Bangkok, of an asylum seeker trapped outside Calais, or of an unemployed disabled adult rendered homeless by the rolling out of Universal Credit in the UK, can be comprehensive or complete in the absence of meso- and macro-theories of the contexts and circumstances in which people experience shame and/or blame.

Third, I shall argue that any sociology worth its salt must address issues of transformative policy and practice, and this is a logical and a moral 'must'. Appropriate disciplinary outcomes cannot be captured in institutionalised metrics of productivity dwelling on the likes of funded projects, media exposure and articles in high-impact journals. Rather, sociology is *necessarily* allied with what Habermas (1984, 1987) calls 'lifeworld rationalisation', namely a responsibility to inform and galvanise public deliberation and action. It is not enough to document, publish and retreat or move on. I develop the notions of 'foresight' and 'action sociology' introduced elsewhere (Scambler, 2018a). The former refers to postulating and exploring possible 'alternative futures', the latter to an evidence-based commitment to securing a rationalisation of the lifeworld sufficient to allow for the challenging and righting of intolerable wrongs.

To lend continuity to the text, subsequent chapters will sporadically feature discussions of four groups in particular: migrants/refugees; the long-term sick and/or disabled; the homeless; and sex workers. For each, the stigma/deviance dialectic has a special, personal and painful relevance. It will suffice here to give brief introductions to these groups.

Migrants/Refugees

Movement around the globe is breaking historical records, both in absolute numbers and in proportions of (national) populations. The 'push and pull' factors at work are varied but there is no doubting the causal role of climate change and shifting ecological systems, geopolitics, wars, and absolute and relative poverty. Definitions of migrants are resonant of these causal factors, but have also become increasingly 'weaponised' for political purposes, as is evidenced by the election of Trump in the USA and the narrow opting for a UKIP-promoted Brexit in the UK. This is especially true of international migration, a term that only too often subsumes, and calculatingly so, asylum seekers in pursuit of places safe from persecution, torture and even state-sanctioned homicide.

A general typology of migration might differentiate between four broad categories:

- *economic* (e.g. to find work);
- *social* (e.g. to be close to family or friends or to enhance the quality of life);
- *political* (e.g. to flee from persecution or war);
- *environmental* (e.g. to escape natural disasters).

In the UK experiencing near-full employment through the 1950s and into the 1960s, economic considerations were to the fore. Moreover, pull factors were augmented by deliberate campaigns to attract workers from the British Commonwealth, initially from the Caribbean and later from India, Pakistan and Bangladesh (i.e. from *New Commonwealth*), to work in textile factories, transport, health or steelworks, often to undertake so-called cellar jobs lacking appeal to native workers. Over time social impulses were appended to the push and pull of economic factors. Exceptionally, East African Asians who had settled in Uganda became political migrants to the UK with the assumption of power of Idi Amin. By the 1970s, however, a UK no longer enjoying either full employment or the growth, let alone prosperity, familiar in the post-war years was beginning to tighten migration controls.

Membership of the European Union (EU) facilitated further bouts of migration. In 1973, the UK joined what was then the European Economic Community (EEC), consisting initially of six states, its membership subsequently being ratified by a referendum in 1975.

The number of member states grew incrementally until, in 2004, Poland and seven other countries joined, once again boosting migration to the UK, with the UK one of three countries to immediately open its borders to workers from the new member states (Polish migrants were in the vanguard). The EU now comprises 28 states, and migration controls within the EU vary from one member state to another. Prior to the 'yes/no' referendum on the UK's continued EU membership in 2016, far-right advocates of Brexit effectively fermented racism among those who judged themselves deprived of jobs, houses and hope by presenting leaving the EU as the sole means of arresting migration to the UK, a process held accountable for the miseries people were enduring. Post-2010 politically motivated policies of 'austerity' barely got a mention. Brexit won the day, with divisive and damaging consequences yet to be resolved.

Of growing pertinence in the twenty-first century in general are political and environmental factors. These are represented in the notion of 'forced migration or displacement'. According to the International Organization for Migration (IOM), forced migration is 'a migratory movement in which an element of coercion exists, whether arising from natural or man-made causes (e.g. movements of refugees and internally displaced persons as well as people displaced by natural or environmental disasters, chemical or nuclear disasters, famine, or developmental projects' (IOM, 2011)). It is estimated that a record 68.5 million people are fleeing war or persecution worldwide, that is, one in 110 people is 'displaced' (Beaumont, 2018). As far as the EU is concerned, and gathering momentum since 2016, an influx of desperate refugees and asylum seekers from the Middle East in general, and Syria in particular, has been seen as specially 'problematic'. At the time of writing, some 34,361 refugees are thought to have died trying to reach the putative security of Europe (McIntyre & Rice-Oxley, 2018). The irony of this will become clear.

So migrants/refugees represent one of the four disparate combinations, or groups, serving as substantive foci for a revised sociology of shame and blame. Enough has surely been said in these few paragraphs to call expectantly on extant sociologies of embodiment and the emotions, of war, of feminist and post-colonial discourses, as well as more obvious resources like stratification, ethnicity, politics and political economy.

Long-Term Sick and Disabled

Chronic or long-term sickness is becoming more common in the UK and globally as people live longer. It is now *the* primary challenge to those concerned with delivering public health and health-care systems. Disability forms an imperfect alliance with long-term sickness. Long-term sickness has long been problematic in so-called developed societies, not least since it typically involves a release from an 'imperative to work' that sits at the core of the ethos and ideology of capitalism. In the UK, generally representative of many kindred Western societies, it was delegated post-World War II to state-sanctioned and culturally recognised experts, physicians, to make the crucial judgement as to whether people with enduring health problems needed time off work. It was doctors in other words who policed attendance at work by adjudicating on people's claims to be sick. More recently in the UK, however, this function has been largely taken from doctors and contracted out to for-profit firms employing non-clinically trained personnel to make such judgements in a government-sponsored attempt to cut 'sick pay' and welfare support.

The tendency to regard long-term illness and/or disability as an individual issue has come to be challenged by disability theorists and activists with increasing vigour and subtlety over the last quarter of the twentieth century. Disability activists rejected the notion that those with disabilities, age-related or otherwise, are victims of a personal, 'tragic' interruption and disruption to an otherwise normal life course, insisting instead on a 'social model'. 'Bad' sickness and disability as opposed to 'good' health, 'bad' abnormality as opposed to 'good' normality, are socially defined and socially accorded value. Moreover, these are contestable attributions anchored in a set of social structures, cultures and institutions that are themselves open to interrogation.

In the UK, one in five people are affected by what Thomas (2012), in pursuit of a neutral term, calls 'impairments' (Papworth Trust, 2013); and less than a fifth of these are born with their impairments. Table 1.1 gives some further details. Unsurprisingly, co-morbidities and disabilities cluster as people get older. Some are more indicative of disadvantage, stigma and outsider status than others. For these ageism can be, and often is, compounded by stigmatisation, ranging from outright rejection and job discrimination through sanctioning and benefit deprivation by contracted for-profit companies to 'blanking' and more subtle interpersonal avoidance like that experienced by Jack Ashley.

Table 1.1 Disability in the UK: some statistics

- Disability affects one in five people (19%) in the UK.
- Only 17% of disabled people are born with their disabilities.
- The prevalence of disability rises with age: in 2011–2012, 6% of children were disabled, 16% of adults of working age and 45% of adults over state pension age.
- Disabled people are less likely to be in employment: in 2013, the UK employment rate for working age disabled people was 49%, compared to 82% of non-disabled people.
- The two most commonly stated enablers of employment for adults with impairments are flexible hours/days and tax credits.
- The two most common barriers to work among adults with impairments are a lack of job opportunities (43%) and difficulty with transport (29%).
- Aged 18, disabled young people are more likely than their non-disabled peers to not be in any form of education, employment or training (NEET): 22% compared to 15%.
- The Internet has become a key tool for those looking for work, but in 2013 one-third (33%) of disabled people had never used the Internet: disabled people are four times more likely to have never used the Internet than non-disabled people.
- 19% of households that include a disabled person live in relative income poverty, compared to 15% of those without a disabled person.
- Disabled people's living costs are 25% higher than those of non-disabled people.
- The majority of impairments are not visible: less than 8% of disabled people use wheelchairs.
- Around 15% of households that contained one or more disabled persons felt their current home was not suitable for their needs and required adaptations.
- Transport is the largest concern for disabled people in their local area: pavement/road maintenance, access and frequency of public transport are the biggest issues.
- More than 20% of disabled people have experienced harassment in public because of their impairment.

- Nine out of 10 people with a learning disability have been victims of hate crime and bullying.
- The annual cost of bringing up a disabled child is three times greater than that of bringing up a non-disabled child.
- About 60% of children and young people with both learning difficulties and mental ill health live in poverty.
- One in 4 people will experience mental ill health in any given year.
- Over one in 4 disabled people say that they frequently do not have choice and control over their daily lives.
- Disabled people are likely to be under-represented in public life: in 2012–2013, one in 5 people were disabled, but only around 5% of public appointments and reappointments were filled by disabled people.
- The WHO has predicted that depression will be the leading cause of disability by 2020.

Adapted from Papworth Trust (2013) (see Scambler, 2018b)

Homeless

Historically, there has always been a small homeless 'vagrant' fraction in Western populations. In the UK, it was an inconspicuous minority until the Thatcher, and 'Thatcherite', 1980s; and since 2010, it has grown exponentially. The statistics back up my personal observations over time in London: my first academic appointment as a Research Associate at St Bartholomew's Hospital was in 1972 and I remained a commuter, latterly at UCL, until retiring in 2013 (and have I have visited weekly subsequently). Rare—and more tolerated—outsider presences adjacent to underground stations have translated into multiple—less tolerated—pleas for loose change at regular intervals along London's major highways. Finding spots to sleep has become a skill in its own right, with hostels often deemed risk environments and many homeless-friendly public spaces being purposively 'armed' by spikes. The homeless have for many become workshy, 'skiving' beggars.

Definitions and legal responsibilities vary. In England, there has for some time been no statutory duty on councils to house everyone who becomes homeless, but they *must* find somewhere for a person to live if they are demonstrably 'vulnerable', as in the case of families with children or after an emergency such as a flood or fire (though this is about to change and soon councils will be theoretically obligated to prevent and relieve homelessness for everyone). Temporary accommodation while people's claims for assistance are assessed or they are waiting for somewhere suitable, can take the form of B&Bs, hostels or private rentals. Rough sleeping—infrequently on the streets—is a separate and distinctive social phenomenon. Accurate figures are difficult to obtain, but this is undoubtedly on the rise. It is estimated that there has been a rise of 169% since 2010 (and of 15% from 2016 to 2017): the figure for autumn 2017 has been put at 4751 sleeping rough on any one night in England, but this is in all probability a severe underestimate. Perhaps predictably, it was the North West of England that saw the sharpest percentage increase in rough sleeping in 2017 (39%), followed by the East Midlands (23%) and Yorkshire and Humber (20%) (www.homeless.org.uk, 2018).

The homeless in general, and rough sleepers in particular, are classic outsiders. Moreover, data on the true extent of their vulnerability are now becoming both available and more accessible. An investigation by the *Guardian* revealed that the number of people recorded dying on streets or in temporary accommodation has more than doubled over the past five years in the UK. People have been found dead in supermarket car parks, church graveyards and crowded hostels. The number of deaths has risen year on year, from 31 in 2013 to 70 in 2017 (with at least 230 dying over that period). The authors of this piece concluded that this is likely to be a significant underestimate as no part of the UK government records homeless death statistics at a national level, and local authorities are not required to count rough sleeper deaths. The average age of a rough sleeper death was 43, nearly half the UK life expectancy (Greenfield & Marsh, 2018). These sparse statistics for England and the UK, mere 'guesstimates', tell little of a compelling story of outsider suffering: sub-zero temperatures in makeshift beds of rags and newspapers, insults and worse from passers-by, being 'moved on' by local police forces anxious to cleanse the streets for tourists and 'special events'.

SEX WORKERS

Definitions of sex work, a more accurate as well as respectful nomenclature than prostitution, tend to be far-reaching, in the UK extending to all those who offer sexual services for any kind of remuneration, goods or services. As with migrants and refugees and the homeless, we are reliant on 'best guesses' as to numbers. This is in part a function of the sheer heterogeneity of a sub-population wrongly stereotyped as homogeneous, plus the fact that definitions often reflect moral stances 'for-or-against'. It is a population that includes individuals who work only very occasionally, perhaps to earn money to fund a decent Christmas for their children, to those who fashion long-term careers (maybe by switching to 'special services' like sadomasochistic practices as they enter middle age). Male sex workers are frequently overlooked, despite the fact that more than one in three sex workers in London are male, and 'trans', 'shemales', 'ladyboys' often go missing altogether. Those resolutely against sex work tend to exaggerate elements of sex trafficking. While sex trafficking certainly exists, and its difficult to see why and how it might be defended, those who regard all sex workers as victims are prone to see all migrant sex workers as necessarily trafficked; in fact, in the UK the evidence suggests that very few migrant sex workers have been trafficked. There is a tendency too to focus on and condemn sex trafficking rather than human trafficking per se.

There exists a hierarchy of prestige in sex work, despite the fact that sex workers themselves sometimes decry such differentiation. But putative differences in prestige are associated with commensurate differences in earning potential. Street workers typically earn the least, notwithstanding how hard they work and the fortitude they show. Those who work in brothels—legally or illegally: it remains illegal for two or more persons to work simultaneously from the same premises—or from flats come next; while those who work from and for escort agencies (agencies typically take a third of the fees a client pays) tend to fare better; and the privileged few, top models who work anonymously and discretely for madams, can earn considerably more.

Unsurprisingly, the monetary rewards on offer are the key motivation for recruitment to the sex industry. Contexts vary however: while for some short-term gains are essential to feed drug use, for others calculating decisions are opportunistically taken to accumulate sufficient savings to transform otherwise hopeless life chances (Scambler, 2007). But finance is not the only factor affecting recruitment. Sex work can run in families; it can be triggered by peer contact; and it can deliver freedom and autonomy around the upbringing, schooling and care of young children.

Clients are overwhelmingly men, but they come from all walks of life and there are estimates that more than one in ten of all adult males in the

UK have at one time or another paid for sexual services. It goes without saying that only those with high incomes can afford to consort with workers charging in excess of £1000 per night or to take them abroad on holidays (sometimes on business expenses). Client motivations too are more complex than many suspect. Added to 'sex uncomplicated by the nuts and bolts of a relationship', maybe incorporating clandestine fantasies like spanking or domination, are the likes of sex addiction, broken relationships, loneliness and the despair of ever having a partner. There are sex workers who offer their services exclusively to people with disabilities.

The chapters that follow refer to and develop theories around stigma and stigmatisation with reference to these four subpopulations, largely but not exclusively in the UK. Firstly, a general theoretical frame is outlined. Starting from the justly influential but increasingly queried account of Goffman (1968) and extending to insider/outsider analyses advanced by theorists from non-interactionist schools of sociology like figurational sociology, a series of themes that inform and shape subsequent chapters are laid out. The frame with which the chapter concludes, owing much to critical theory and critical realism, forms the conceptual basis on which Chapters 3–6 build.

Chapter 3 deploys Habermas' (1984, 1987) distinction between system and lifeworld to consider the minutiae of shame and blame in the latter. How, I ask, do these normative intrusions into the day-to-day conduct of affairs play out in people's sense of self and of others. What is it like to be 'othered'? Here, the causal interplay of agency, culture and structure is confronted. They are also re-theorised by reference not only to Habermasian critical theory but also to the critical realism of Bhaskar and Archer. Illustrations are forthcoming from the substantive literature on the marginalised groups under scrutiny.

In Chapter 4, the focus is on ways in which macro- and micro-theories might be optimally linked via the fostering of meso- or middle-range theories. A series of meso-theories around stigma and deviance and the insider/outsider binary are promulgated. Theorising of this sort, it is maintained, is the very lifeblood of professional sociology. Accent is placed on the salience of what I call *metareflection*, namely the mining of extant theory and research from across and beyond the discipline of sociology: the core contention here is that sociologists are under pressure to 'compress the past', to neglect past/historical scholarly accomplishments in favour of up-to-date publications, in the process reinventing many a wheel. Links are explored here between the latest phase of 'financialised' capitalism and the flotsam and jetsam of everyday interaction.

Chapter 5 revisits the notion that the social and sociological can never 'wrap up' or decisively conclude causal analyses of *any* social phenomena. This is: (a) because biological, psychological and social mechanisms are always and continuously in play—issuing in what critical realists call 'tendencies'; (b) because one social mechanism can compromise or annul another; (c) because agency and contingency have to be factored in; and (d) because in any 'open system', or society, biological, psychological and social mechanisms, though 'irreducible', do not, it follows from (a) to (c), simply and unambiguously result in observable events.

In Chapter 6, the fruit of the framing and substantive references offered throughout the volume culminate in a revised *sociology of stigma* and new understanding of insider/outsider dynamics for the—many now argue doomed—financial capitalism of the early twenty-first century (Streeck, 2016; Wallerstein et al., 2013). A preliminary test of this 'new understanding' is its capacity to expose and explicate the stigmatised, outsider status of the four subpopulations under scrutiny. In this chapter and the conclusion that succeeds it, an appropriate programme for continuing research is spelled out. This necessarily represents a transnational or global challenge, matched by a global sociology; a global sociology cannot collapse into an occidental sociology writ large.

REFERENCES

Ashley, J. (1973). *Journey into silence*. Oxford: Bodley Head.
Beaumont, P. (2018, June 19). Record 68.5 million people feeling war or persecution worldwide. *The Guardian*.
Goffman, E. (1968). *Stigma: The management of spoiled identity*. Harmondsworth: Penguin.
Greenfield, P., & Marsh, S. (2018). Deaths of UK homeless people more than double in five years. *The Guardian*. www.theguardian.com//society/2018/apr/11/deaths-of-uk-homeless-people-more-than-double-in-five-years.
Habermas, J. (1984). *Theory of communicative action, volume 1: Reason and the rationalization of society*. London: Heinemann.
Habermas, J. (1987). *Theory of communicative action, volume 2: Lifeworld and system: A critique of functionalist reason*. Cambridge: Polity Press.
Homeless.org.uk. (2018). www.homeless.org.uk/facts/homelessness-in-numbers/rough-sleeping-our-analysis.

International Organisation for Migration (IOM). (2011). *Glossary on migration*. http://migrationdataportal.org/themes/forced-migration-or-displacement/. Accessed 16 May 2018.

McIntyre, N., & Rice-Oxley, M. (2018, June 20). The list—It's 34,361 and rising: How the list tallies Europe's migrant bodycount. *The Guardian*.

Papworth Trust. (2013). *Disability in the United Kingdom 2013: Facts and figures*. http://www.papworth.org.uk. Accessed 6 August 2017.

Scambler, G. (2007). Sex work stigma: Opportunist migrants in London. *Sociology, 41*, 1079–1096.

Scambler, G. (2018a). *Sociology, health and the fractured society: A critical realist account*. London: Routledge.

Scambler, G. (2018b). Heaping blame on shame: 'Weaponising stigma' for neoliberal times. *Sociological Review, 66*, 766–782.

Streeck, W. (2016). *How will capitalism end?* London: Verso.

Thomas, C. (2012). Theorizing disability and chronic illness: Where next for perspectives in medical sociology? *Social Theory and Health, 10*, 209–228.

Wallerstein, I., Collins, R., Mann, M., Derluguian, G., & Calhoun, C. (2013). *Does capitalism have a future?* Oxford: Oxford University Press.

Wittgenstein, L. (1958). *Philosophical investigations* (2nd ed.). Oxford: Blackwell.

CHAPTER 2

Theoretical Perspectives on Shame and Blame

Abstract This chapter gives critical consideration to some of the main sociological approaches to, and theories of, stigma. Goffman's work is appraised in some detail and its limitations exposed. This is followed by discussions of other insider/outsider analyses, encompassing the figurational studies of Elias. Themes of the relationships between insiders or the established and outsiders or strangers are explored. Finally, the chapter introduces two types of social theory that inform this investigation, namely critical theory and critical realism.

Keywords Goffman · Elias · Insider/outsider dialectics · Critical theory · Critical realism

The sociological literature on stigma often seems to be caught in a Goffmanesque time warp, though as we shall see there is a whiff of change in the air. Goffman's focus was on the rules governing everyday interactions in what has since been defined as the 'lifeworld'. Like the later Wittgenstein (1958), Goffman afforded full recognition and, as it were, credibility and credit to the subtle structures and practices that comprise the raw materials for our getting by day-to-day. It is worth dwelling briefly on this at the outset, drawing not only on Goffman's classic exegesis in *Stigma: The Management of Spoiled Identity* (1968a), but on his more generic and wide-ranging *The Presentation of Self in Everyday Life* (1969). It is not, I shall contend in this short volume, that Goffman got it wrong, more that there are telling 'absences' in his *dramaturgical* perspective and in the primary focus of his research.

Goffman's primary interest was in the structure of mundane or everyday interaction. His micro-sociological project was to expose the interactional *rules* that, knowingly or otherwise, people follow: these rules, he maintained, regulate interaction. Moreover, the structuring of mundane face-to-face interaction via such rules functions to stabilise the social order. His analyses were termed 'dramaturgical' because he noted that people conduct themselves in the lifeworld much as actors perform in the theatre, that is, in accordance with learned scripts. He specified a number of what he called 'ground rules' that announce the means available to people to accomplish their goals. These provide normative regulation. To cite an instance, one primary ground rule has to do with 'maintenance of face', which requires people—like actors performing on a stage—to present and sustain positive images of the self and to acknowledge the relevance of this same process for those with whom they interact. This is accomplished through 'acting lines': participants in interaction typically act to prevent lines from being discredited, in this way avoiding loss of face for *all* those involved. When push comes to shove, social life is predictable to the extent to which those who interact arrive at a tacit or consensual working definition of the situation.

Definitions of the situation can, and often do, reflect the distribution of power in a group or a society. Goffman found in his study of a psychiatric unit, for example, that an individual's performed self can be, and frequently is, challenged by others proffering a rival definition. The moral? The self, Goffman (1968b) asserts, is not a property of the individual to whom it is attributed, but rather resides 'in the pattern of social control that is exerted in connection with the person by himself and those around him' (note the predictable and sexist phrasing of the patriarchal day). The self, in other words, is the product of *an institutional nexus of performances* (though it should be stressed that the psychiatric unit—an example of what Goffman called a 'total institution'—is an extreme form).

Rule-breaking, Goffman argued, is as important for the maintenance of social order as rule-following. Moreover, rule-breaking, or 'remedial interchanges', is very common. This is because interactional exchanges are structured primarily to allow individuals to 'adjust' while pursuing their personal goals with a minimum of fuss and disruption. Rule-breaking of this type, typically accomplished through 'accounts', 'apologies' or 'requests', gets the traffic moving again (Goffman, 1971). It is generally more felicitous to overlook individuals' rule-breaking than to confront them or hold them to account. In his account of the routine, everyday management of stigma, Goffman developed and elaborated on this general framing of social interaction. Stigma, he rightly insisted, is not an attribute intrinsic to individuals but part of a system of social relations:

> the term stigma, then, will be used to refer to an attribute that is deeply discrediting, but it should be seen that a language of relationships, not attributes, is really needed. An attribute that stigmatizes one type of possessor can confirm the usualness of another, and therefore is neither creditable nor discreditable as a thing in itself. (Goffman, 1968a: 13)

Systems of social relations differ by time and place: so an attribute, trait or condition that is stigmatising in one era, society, community or context may not be in another.

People can be *discredited* or *discreditable*. With the former, the stigma is obvious and cannot be concealed, as with a conspicuous disability for example. In such instances, the problem for its possessor is the management of the—often stereotypical—impressions that others have of her or him and the behaviour they anticipate or predict in consequence. With the latter, the stigma is inconspicuous and therefore the option to conceal it—to 'pass as normal'—arises. The problem for its possessor here is the management of information: who to tell, when, how and with what consequences.

Goffman discerned three basic types of stigma. The first is associated with 'abominations of the body' or 'the various physical deformities'. The second denotes 'blemishes of individual character' interpreted as 'weakness of will, domineering or unnatural passions, treacherous and rigid beliefs, and dishonesty, these being inferred from a known record of, for example, mental disorder, imprisonment, addiction, alcoholism, homosexuality, unemployment, suicidal attempts, and radical political behaviour'. And third come tribal stigmas linked to race, nation and religion that can be 'transmitted through lineages and equally contaminate all members of a family' (Goffman, 1968a: 14). What we 'normals' do in relation to people caught up in one or other of this triad, Goffman averred, is construct a stigma theory or ideology to account for their 'inferiority' and the danger they represent, on occasions and often unthinkingly rationalising an animosity rooted in other differences, such as those of social class.

Goffman's principal commitment was to analysing in meticulous detail the lifeworld transactions—the dynamics of the presentation of self in the specific context of 'spoiled identities'—in which the stigmatised inevitably become involved. The additional concepts he introduces will feature in discussions throughout this book and do not require rehearsal at this point. What I want to do instead is to highlight key criticisms of his work. To reiterate, while I think these significant and compelling they do not in my view render Goffman's *sensitisation* of the concept of stigma redundant. It will be readily apparent that there is much in his work that speaks to the lived experience of members of the four groups—migrants/refugees, the long-term sick/disabled, the homeless and sex workers—selected for special attention.

Goffman's Limitations

One of the most significant planks of Durkheim's contribution to the genesis of sociological investigation was his (methodologically holist) insistence on the discipline's pursuit of 'social facts'; indeed, he viewed sociology as the empirical study of social facts. Social facts here comprise the values, norms and structures that transcend individuals and can exercise constraint and control over them. For him concepts like social class cannot be reduced to what individuals think and do. Even what strike as uniquely individual acts, like suicide, must be broached sociologically as irreducibly social. Social facts act on individuals as 'externally' constraining and/or controlling. Durkheim here paves for a general and pervasive criticism of Goffman's input on stigma. It is not just that his point of interest is the micro-sociology of social/dramaturgical exchange. It is rather that it is misleading and unacceptable to ignore or neglect 'external' macro- and meso-social constraints/controls on the lifeworld. Interestingly, Tyler (2018) has recently noted that Goffman actively resisted, even condemned, attempts to broach macro- and meso-, and especially macro- and meso-*political*, phenomena in the name of sociological endeavour.

One way of illustrating the importance of Durkheimian social facts is via the figurational sociology of Elias (2000). Elias specialised in the long-term unfolding of social phenomena and their often unheralded and gradual insinuation into people's lives. He framed this in terms of specific contexts or 'figurations'. Figurations stand for evolving networks of interdependent humans (Quintaneiro, 2004). It is 'process' that acts as the magnet for Elias, who was particularly interested in the connections between shifts in macro- and meso-social structures on the one hand and psychological aspects of personhood on the other. Notable here is *The Established and the Outsiders* (Elias & Scotson, 2008), which lends itself to an interrogation of Goffmanesque and companion interactionist analyses. It is of special pertinence to the increasingly topical issue of migration and the plight of refugees.

So how might Elias' figurational approach cause us to query and amend Goffman's dramaturgical focus? I maintain that Elias' theorising epitomises what is absent in Goffman's. The work that witnessed the light of day in *The Established and the Outsiders* was done by Scotson under Elias' supervision. It reported (their) research on a local community on the outskirts of Leicester that they named 'Winston Parva'. They focused on three groups in particular: the first comprised established village families who had been in Winston Parva for several generations and were predominantly working class; the second consisted of middle-class families who had moved into the neighbourhood to occupy newly built housing; and the third, mostly working class, were newcomers residing in a different segment of the village. The results of the study were unanticipated. They found that relationships *across all the groups* were characterised by material exclusion and by social exclusion via gossip, group disgrace and social control. As outsiders, they were stigmatised as unclean and deviant, leading to 'us' versus 'them' representations and enactments (Smith, 2001). Most significant therefore was the binary: established 'versus' outsiders. The former were characterised by strong social cohesion and networks and shared backgrounds, while the latter comprised novitiates who were essentially strangers to each other and lacked access to significant networks and influential (institutional) positions (Petintseva, 2015).

Elias was interested in how power is exercised. He concluded that although material and economic inequalities play their part, power cannot and must not be *reduced* to them. Power is relational and dynamic. Like Weber, he applauded Marx's contribution, largely accepting the weight of modes of production on power relations and class formation; but he went on to insist that symbolic factors and status also have their input, the more so when power balances are uneven. He left ample room, in other words, for 'socio-psychological processes (the creation of group identity, labelling, emotions)' (Petintseva, 2015: 7). Moreover, Elias also took issue with overly simple emphases on social structures as causal mechanisms. Ethnicity, for example, is for him an *outcome* of the unequal distribution of power, not what actually determines people's positions and relations in the first place.

Outsiders for Elias comprise groups that do not have the requisite social networks and can expect to meet with intolerance, suspicion and possibly more blunt modes of rejection and control. The established, on the other hand, enjoy access to power resources denied to outsiders from the outset. They can mobilise these resources to 'other' outsiders, to keep them 'in their place' and to re-affirm the position of their own group: they develop a kind of collective fantasy that justifies their aversion to outsider groups as well as their own superordinate status (Stanley, 2017). Elias' established–outsiders figurations, it is important to note, require us to look beyond: (a) the assumptions of absolute and one-sided exclusion and (b) the typical dualities of rationality or irrationality. His figurational sociology seeks to escape from each of Dawe's (1970) 'two sociologies', the one led by the concept of agency and the other by that of structure. Goffman is contextualised, not abandoned.

Fortuitously, a number of authors have also made direct links to migrants and refugees (Petintseva, 2015; Stanley, 2017). Petintseva, for example, has interrogated the relevance of Elias' established–outsiders analysis for understanding the circumstances of 'new migrants' to Western Europe. She delineates four dimensions to the process of outsidering these escapees:

- the relatively powerless position: in economic terms, but also in terms of access to social or formal facilities, services or institutions (e.g. legal status, possibilities of mobility, status differentials in institutional contexts);
- the lack of protection and opportunities afforded by membership in powerful social networks;
- limited internal cohesion between new migrants as a whole, rooted in the fact that they are all 'new' (Petintseva argues here that Elias' analysis needs to be 'de-localised', so an example here would be the possibility of resisting in terms of a political voice);
- representations and stereotypes of these groups as threatening, images based on the socially unacceptable characteristics of a small minority of group members (e.g. issues of social distancing, 'ethicizing' and problematising particular attributes).

The degree to which these 'signs' are present, Pentintseva maintains, defines the extent to which migrant groups can be regarded as 'new' in terms of Elias' established—outsiders dichotomy *in particular circumstances*. Her approach, she contends, opens the way for researchers 'to trace the processes of *outsidering* in daily practices, lived realities and subtle discourses, in micro-contexts but also at the institutional and state level' (Pentintseva, 2015: 11).

The salience of Elias' theoretical and conceptual armoury, together with Pentitseva's amendments, for a credible sociology of the shaming and blaming of migrants and refugees is apparent. Goffman's micro-sociology is not lost, but rather revised and complemented by theories derived from meso-theory, and to a lesser extent macro-sociology. The chapters that follow build on the contributions of Goffman and Elias among others, but it is the task of the next two sections to provide a more sturdy scaffolding for the arguments that follow. The first engages in some philosophical 'under-labouring', in the process introducing critical realism, as exemplified in the work of Roy Bhaskar, and critical theory, as developed by Jurgen Habermas. The second and concluding section of this chapter anticipates a sociological theory of shame and blame that is the beneficiary of critical realist/critical theoretical perspectives and underpins the analyses to come.

CRITICAL REALISM

In the paragraphs that follow, I limit myself to laying out some core tenets of what has grown into an ambitious project (see Scambler, 2018). The question of what *exists*, Bhaskar (2016) argued, has gone missing from much of Western philosophy. In fact, this question has been reduced to another: What can we *know* of what exists? Ontology has been reduced to epistemology. Bhaskar called this the 'epistemic fallacy'. He sought to rehabilitate ontology. He drew distinctions between *experience*, the *events* that experience makes accessible to us, and what he termed the *real*, referring to those generative or causal mechanisms that *must* exist if the events with which we are familiar are to be accounted for or explained. It is the task of both the natural and social sciences to discover and expose these mechanisms. But while the natural sciences can often deploy laboratory-style experiments—that is, can secure 'closures'—in what is otherwise a complex and dynamic world, or 'open system', the social sciences have typically to rely on what Bhaskar calls 'retroductive inferences' from the 'demi-regularities' deriving from quantitative research, or what he calls 'abductive inferences' deriving from qualitative or ethnographic research. All scientific knowledge of the world remains fallible, or liable to future revision; but, as will become apparent, the really existing mechanisms inferred from social as well as natural scientific research have considerable stamina.

More will be said about the more abstruse tenets of critical realism as and when required, but it is important for now to illustrate its value to sociological enquiry. It should already be evident that both Goffman's studies of the mundane day-by-day presentation of self and Elias' of the evolving processes of othering outsider groups by the already established expose mechanisms, the former largely at the level of dyadic interactional encounters and the latter largely at the level of group dynamics. I shall argue in the final section of this chapter for a critical realist approach—oriented to mechanisms—to account for extant practices of shaming and blaming. In the meantime, it will be sufficient to put just a little flesh on the skeleton. Consider the plethora of refugees currently fleeing Syria, the Yemen and other Middle-Eastern 'failed states' and heading for the EU, or the caravan of thousands in flight from central American states and at the time of writing crossing Mexico en route to the USA. While Goffman's and Elias' accounts retain their purchase for these groups, it is abundantly clear that there is quite another genus of mechanisms involved.

No credible explanation for the flights of these refugees could neglect the macro-sociology of Middle-Eastern interstate conflict, the geopolitical and commercial strategies of the leading Western powers (extending to the unwavering sponsorship of Israel), or the often prepotent commitment of Western and other countries' theocracies, autocracies, governing oligarchies or plutocracies to secure the acquiescence/support/votes of their peoples. To accept this much is to sign up to the search for mechanisms at the level of the world-system. So while the analyses of Goffman and more obviously Elias (e.g. relations between established EU/US citizenry, groups and institutions and refugees or 'strangers' expediently recast as economic migrants) still have resonance, much of the story is untold.

This has important ramifications for viable sociological accounts of the long-term sick and disabled, the homeless and sex workers as well as for migrants and refugees. No plausible sociology of shame and blame can afford to ignore a vast array of mechanisms that comprise three *tiers*:

from analyses of micro-phenomena of the kind provided by Goffman, through those of meso-phenomena as exemplified by Elias, to studies of macro-phenomena like systems of stratification, governance and culture now breaking free or leaking out of nation states to span the globe.

But critical realist philosophy alerts us to further complications. It is not just that mechanisms have to be retroductively or abductively inferred from research data, or even that they operate at each of the three tiers of micro, meso and macro. Mechanisms in the realm of the social:

- rarely manifest themselves straightforwardly in events or phenomena of interest to sociologists;
- can be structural, cultural *or agential*;
- remain active—as 'tendencies'—independently of any degree of causal responsibility for such events or phenomena;
- can have their causal powers or potentials nudged aside or bypassed by other mechanisms (e.g. agency subdued by structure or culture, class mitigated or neutralised by gender or ethnicity);
- though irreducible to them, are nevertheless responsive to ('emergent from') biological and psychological mechanisms (i.e. the possession of appropriate cells and aptitude are prerequisites for winning Wimbledon, but it is people who compete at this social event);
- allowance has always to be made for happenstance and contingency.

All this is less forbidding and depressing than it might appear. What it amounts to is an acknowledgement that the sociological project of discerning, describing and explaining social phenomena, and linking them to compose a narrative of social order and change, *can only assist, and that fallibly, in addressing of the human condition in what is ineluctably an open system.*

CRITICAL THEORY

If critical realism commends many brands of 'realism', then critical *theory* allows for a more discrete and substantive input. I shall not here trace its ancestry in the works of Marx and the early Frankfurt School (see Scambler, 2001, 2018), but rather settle on a key distinction made by Habermas (1984, 1987), namely that between 'system' and 'lifeworld'.

This distinction serves two functions in subsequent chapters: first, it characterises a continuing tension in financial capitalism, and second, it has utility as a conceptual and heuristic device. The lifeworld for Habermas is the everyday world of sociability that we inhabit and within which we interact and form relationships rooted—generally—in trust and reciprocity, that is, characterised by what Habermas calls 'communicative action' or action oriented to consensus (Goffman's territory). People's use of language implies a common endeavour to attain consensus in a context in which all participants are free to contribute and have equal opportunities to do so. Language use, in short, presupposes a commitment to an *ideal speech situation* in which discourse can reach its full potential. It is a claim that recognises no historical limitations. The idea of rationally motivated shared understanding—and rational motivation implies a total lack of compulsion or manipulation—is, Habermas, maintains, built into the very reproduction of social life. The symbolic reproduction of social life is based on the 'counterfactual' ideal of the ideal speech situation, which is characterised by 'communicative symmetry' and a compulsion-free consensus (see Scambler, 1996).

The lifeworld can be contrasted with the system. This denotes the role of economy and state and is characterised by 'strategic action', or action oriented to outcome. Modernity, referring to the post-Enlightenment or modern world, has witnessed a differentiation of both lifeworld and system into distinct spheres and, more significantly, a discernible 'de-coupling' of lifeworld and system. Moreover, the latter has come to 'colonise' the former. How is this to be interpreted? Habermas divides each of lifeworld and system into two sectors, as represented in Table 2.1. The private sector of the lifeworld, epitomised by the household, generates *commitment*. The public sector of the lifeworld, at the time of Habermas' writing more or less exclusively the domain of newspapers and television, gives rise to *influence*. The economic sector of the system, incorporating a range of global markets, acts through its steering media of *money*. Finally, the state sector of the system, featuring a long-armed legal and bureaucratic apparatus, is where *power* derives and is deployed. Habermas' point about colonisation is that the strategic, outcome-oriented system has, through its steering media of money and power, come progressively in modernity to impose itself on, even dictate to, the mundane communicative action, oriented to consensus, of the lifeworld. Commitment and influence have in the process become manipulated and perverted, or more bluntly, bought and regulated.

Table 2.1 Lifeworld and system

Lifeworld	System
(Communicative action)	(Strategic action)
Private sphere	**Economy**
(e.g. household)	(e.g. markets)
Steering media = COMMITMENT	Steering media = MONEY
Public sphere	**State**
(e.g. mainstream media)	(e.g. bureaucracy)
Steering media = INFLUENCE	Steering media = POWER

A singular virtue of Habermas' analyses is that they engage with and promote sociological linkages across the tiers of macro, meso and micro. For example, he translates the macro-phenomena of lifeworld/system decoupling, and the subsequent colonisation of lifeworld by system, into an examination and theorisation of everyday interactional exchanges. He shows how the taken-for-granted communicative ethos can be subverted by strategic action. He writes first of 'open' strategic action: this occurs when money and/or power are explicitly, conspicuously and tellingly on display to demand acquiescence and consent. 'Concealed' strategic action can take two principal forms: (a) 'distorted communication', or manipulation, when one party to an exchange is being strategic and disguises this from the other; and (b) 'systematically distorted communication', when both parties to an exchange are acting in good faith but one party is unwittingly acting strategically, for example, in accordance with an agenda about which he/she is unaware or non-reflexive. In this way, Habermas facilitates the examination of the impact of social transformation and change on routine encounters and conversation. Many an exchange between would-be migrants and refugees and politicians, civil servants, NGOs, border guards, charity workers, protestors and so on can be illuminated via these Habermasian concepts.

A Frame for a Theory of Shame and Blame

Passing reference was made in the Introduction to a distinction between stigma and deviance, the former involving an infringement against cultural norms of shame and the latter an infringement against cultural norms of blame. As it is a distinction that frames and informs much of the analysis that follows, it is timely to elaborate here. I understand stigma to entail an *ontological deficit*. It is not that a person said to possess a stigmatising condition, trait or attribute has 'done something wrong', rather that he/she is in some sense 'imperfect'. It is his or her 'being' that is socially unacceptable and occasions social distancing and 'othering' (this is actually quite close to Goffman's definition). Deviance on the other hand entails a *moral deficit*. Here, culpability is central: the individual is regarded as 'at fault' and therefore fully deserving of any sanctions or punishments. It will be immediately apparent that cultural norms of shame and blame vary by time and place, as we shall see in later discussions of migrants/refugees, the long-term sick/disabled, the homeless and sex workers. Indeed, such variation can occur from neighbourhood to neighbourhood, community to community: context is all.

In Table 2.2, the basic distinction between stigma and deviance is extended to incorporate *enacted*, *felt* and *project* stigma and deviance. Enacted stigma and deviance denote actual discrimination on the grounds of perceived ontological and moral deficits, respectively; felt stigma and deviance refer an internalised sense of shame and blame respectively, plus, critically, a fear of meeting with actual discrimination; finally, project stigma and deviance signal an explicit rejection of enacted and felt stigma and deviance, respectively, and a purposeful intent to resist and counter them. These distinctions derived from an earlier study of mine into how people come to terms with the experience of recurrent seizures and subsequent diagnosis of epilepsy (Scambler, 1989). Over 90% of a community sample spontaneously defined epilepsy as stigmatising, allowing me to follow up with a series of questions and probes. The end product was what I termed the 'hidden distress model of epilepsy'. People with epilepsy are typically discreditable rather than discredited and hence often have the option of non-disclosure and concealment of their seizures/diagnosis. Most people elected this option. As a result,

Table 2.2 Notions of stigma and deviance

Stigma (offences against norms of shame)	**Deviance** (offences against norms of blame)
Enacted stigma	**Enacted deviance**
Actual discrimination (shaming)	Actual discrimination (blaming)
Felt stigma	**Felt deviance**
Fear of discrimination and sense of shame	Fear of discrimination and sense of blame
Project stigma	**Project deviance**
Active resistance to enacted and felt stigma	Active resistance to enacted and felt deviance

the opportunities for others to discriminate against them were seriously diminished. It transpired in fact that felt stigma was much more disruptive of the lives of most people with epilepsy than enacted stigma, hence the naming of the model. Project stigma was discernible in the sample, but I did not really pick up on it at the time and it has generally been neglected in studies of long-term illness and disability. The distinction between stigma and deviance came later.

It will be argued that differentiating stigma and deviance, shame and blame, is pivotal for developing an adequate sociological account that spans micro- to macro-strata in the present era of financial capitalism. The account that unfolds will be built on both critical realist and critical theoretical foundations. It will seek to identify generative/causal mechanisms operative at each of the three tiers of micro, meso and macro with a view to postulating a series of theories linking the systemic transition to financial capitalism in the mid-1970s to the wilful political *weaponising of stigma*—in effect, appending blame to shame—and the impact of these processes, via the kind of meso- or middle-range theories commended long ago by Merton, on the more intimate lifeworld dynamic of group and dyadic encounters. Bhaskar philosophy and Habermas' social theory donate the skeleton onto which the flesh of a theory of shame and blame might be added. In the concluding paragraphs of the book, a revised paradigm or research programme will be sketched.

REFERENCES

Bhaskar, R. (2016). *Enlightened common sense: The philosophy of critical realism.* London: Routledge.
Dawe, A. (1970). The two sociologies. *British Journal of Sociology, 21,* 207–218.
Elias, N. (2000). *The civilising process: Sociogenetic and psychogenetic investigations.* Oxford: Blackwell.
Elias, N., & Scotson, J. (2008). *The established and the outsiders.* Dublin: University of Dublin Press.
Goffman, E. (1968a). *Stigma: The management of spoiled identity.* Harmondsworth: Penguin.
Goffman, E. (1968b). *Asylums: Essays on the social situation of mental patients and other inmates.* Harmondsworth: Penguin.
Goffman, E. (1969). *The presentation of self in everyday life.* Harmondsworth: Penguin.
Goffman, E. (1971). *Relations in public: Microstudies of the social order.* New York: Basic Books.

Habermas, J. (1984). *Theory of communicative action, volume 1: Reason and the rationalization of society.* London: Heinemann.
Habermas, J. (1987). *Theory of communicative action, volume 2: Lifeworld and system: A critique of functionalist reason.* Cambridge: Polity Press.
Petintseva, O. (2015). *Approaching new migration through Elias' 'established' and 'outsider' lens.* https://lib.umich.edu/h/humfig/11217607.0004.304/-approaching-new-migration-through-eliass-established?rgn=main;view=fulltext. Accessed 4 October 2018.
Quintaneiro, T. (2004). The concept of figuration or configuration in Norbert Elias' sociological theory. *Teoria & Sociedade, 12*, 54–69.
Scambler, G. (1989). *Epilepsy.* London: Tavistock.
Scambler, G. (1996). The 'project of modernity' and the parameters for a critical sociology: An argument with illustrations from medical sociology. *Sociology, 30*, 567–581.
Scambler, G. (Ed.). (2001). *Habermas, critical theory and health.* London: Routledge.
Scambler, G. (2018). *Sociology, health and the fractured society: A critical realist account.* London: Routledge.
Smith, D. (2001). *Norbert Elias and modern social theory.* London: Sage.
Stanley, L. (2017). *Whites writing whiteness.* http://www.whiteswritingwhiteness.ed.ac.uk/thinking-with-elias/the-established-outsider-figuration-race-and-whiteness/. Accessed 4 October 2018.
Tyler, I. (2018). Resituating Erving Goffman: From stigma power to black power. *Sociological Review, 66*, 744–765.
Wittgenstein, L. (1958). *Philosophical investigations* (2nd ed.). Oxford: Blackwell.

CHAPTER 3

Asymmetric Lifeworld Encounters

Abstract This chapter gives an expository account of Habermas' basic distinction between the lifeworld on the one hand and the system on the other. The focus is on how attributions of shame and blame play out in people's day-to-day lives. What is it like to be 'othered', to be rendered unacceptable or rejected by 'normals' or 'normal host communities'? The chapter also uses Bhaskar's critical realism in relation to agency, culture and structure to emphasise the causal roots of stigma and deviance, of social norms of shame and blame.

Keywords Habermas · Lifeworld · System · Norms of shame and blame · Bhaskar · Causal mechanisms

To reiterate a point made earlier, it is not so much that Goffman got things wrong than that his narrow focus on micro-phenomena attenuated and restricted the sociological agenda: it ruled out Durkheimian social facts. Habermas' notion of the lifeworld has been introduced, but parsimoniously. A few more comments are required as a prelude to addressing stigma-related everyday social interactions, the theme of this chapter. The opening section provides such an explication. The bulk of the chapter is then given over to a series of case studies which are then examined in some detail. It is argued that such case studies cannot be either understood or explained sociologically in the absence of the external constraints of macro (via meso) theory.

© The Author(s) 2020
G. Scambler, *A Sociology of Shame and Blame*,
https://doi.org/10.1007/978-3-030-23143-9_3

The Lifeworld Unravelled

It is not enough to define the lifeworld as the sum total of our mundane day-to-day dealings with each other, but few rival generalisations are especially weight-bearing. For example, the lifeworld has to do with *social integration*, whereas the system—constituted by economy and state—addresses *system integration*. But the lifeworld cannot 'be known' since it is the vehicle of all knowing. It is not something that people can step outside to assess or evaluate, although, according to Habermas, elements of the lifeworld can and are called into doubt or 'thematised'—that is, made the subject of disputation as participants attempt to re-establish their definition of the situation as a prerequisite for successful cooperation. The lifeworld can be reproduced through communicative action (oriented to consensual understanding and decision-making), but not through strategic action (oriented to the attainment of particular outcomes). The lifeworld, Habermas argues, should be regarded as the medium, or 'symbolic space', within which culture and personality as well as social integration are sustained and reproduced.

Habermas is undoubtedly correct both in arguing that 'system rationalisation' has outstripped 'lifeworld rationalisation'—in other words, that the former has increasing come to permeate or 'colonise' the latter—and in insisting, against Weber's notion of modernity's 'iron cage' bureaucratisation, that this process of colonisation was not in fact inevitable, and nor is it reversible. Table 3.1 affords a general clarification of the relations between system and lifeworld from the perspective of the former.

Habermas (1990, 1993) deepened his theory of communicative action, the ideal speech situation upon which it is premised, and the lifeworld via his 'discourse ethics', and this is of relevance here. He introduced a *principle of universalisation* (which represents a 'socialisation' of Kant's individualistic moral theory). This principle evoked the 'universal exchange of roles' termed 'ideal role-taking' or universal discourse by Mead. Thus, every valid norm has to fulfil the following conditions: '*all* affected can accept the consequences and the side effects its *general* observance can be anticipated to have for the satisfaction of *everyone's* interests (and these consequences are preferred to those of known alternative possibilities for regulation)' (Habermas, 1990: 66; Scambler, 2001).

The principle of universalisation is different from the principle of discourse ethics, which states that 'only those norms can claim to be valid that meet (or could meet) with the approval of all affected in their

Table 3.1 Relations between system and lifeworld from a system perspective

Institutional orders of the lifeworld	Interchange relations	Media-steered subsystems
Private sphere	1) P -----------------------→ Labour power M ←----------------------- Employment income 2) M ←----------------------- Goods and services M -----------------------→ Demand	Economy
Public sphere	1a M -----------------------→ Taxes P ←----------------------- Organisational accomplishments P ←----------------------- Political decision P ----------------------- -→ Mass loyalty	
M = money medium	P = Power medium	

Adapted from Habermas (1987)

capacity *as participants in a practical discourse*' (Habermas, 1990: 66). While the principle of universalisation concerns *moral* questions of 'justice' and 'solidarity', which admit of formal universal resolution, the principle of discourse ethics concerns *ethical* questions of the 'good life', which can only be addressed in the context of substantive cultures, forms of life or individual projects (Scambler, 2001).

Habermas (1996) built on his discourse ethics to address issues of the law and democracy, again matters of import here. He defended a proceduralist conception of deliberative democracy in which the burden of legitimating state power is borne by informal and legally institutionalised processes of political deliberation. This derives from 'the radical democratic idea that the legitimacy of political authority can only be secured through broad popular participation in political deliberation and decision-making or, more succinctly, that there is an internal relation between the rule of law and popular sovereignty' (Cronin & De Greiff, 1998: vii). This, he averred, preserved what is best in both classical liberalism, accenting pre-politically grounded rights of individual liberty, and communitarianism, focused on those culturally transmitted values that form the inescapable background against which all questions of political justice must be resolved.

Habermas went on to spell out those basic rights free and equal citizens must confer on one another if they are to regulate their common life by means of positive law. These rights fall into a number of categories. One set comprises fundamental negative liberties: these are those membership rights and due-process rights that in combination underpin private autonomy. Next come those rights of political participation that guarantee public autonomy. Finally, there are social welfare rights that are necessary for the effective exercise of civil and political rights in that citizens can only input if their basic material needs are met.

So for Habermas the legitimacy of legal norms is a function of those formal properties of procedures of political deliberation and decision-making that support the presumption that their outcomes are rational. The requisite institutions must meet specifiable criteria. There must be, first, a public sphere of open political discussion, characterised by inputs of expert knowledge and by open access to print and electronic media, and institutionally underwritten by the voluntary associations of civil society. The public sphere must be complemented, second, by a legally regulated government apparatus consisting of legislative, judicial and administrative branches. It is a model which according to Cronin and

De Greiff (1998: xvii) involves the 'circulation of power': 'on the input side, influence generated in the public sphere is transformed through the democratic procedures of elections and parliamentary opinion- and will-formation into communicative power; which in turn is transformed through legal programmes and policies of parliamentary bodies into administrative power; at the output end, administrative programmes create the necessary conditions for the existence of civil society and its voluntary associations, and hence of a vibrant political public sphere'.

While it should be axiomatic that this compressed elaboration of the Habermasian theoretical and conceptual framework has considerable traction for a sociology of shame and blame, there is no question that it is also an invitation to critique. The most cursory of unprejudiced reflections on the lot of *each of* migrants and refugees, the long-term sick and disabled, the homeless and sex workers in the UK (and elsewhere) in twenty-first-century financial capitalism testifies to the permeability of the border between the lifeworld and the system and to the brutal realities of system rationalisation and colonisation.

People's Definitions of Their Situations: Foodbanks

It has become a sociological cliché that if a situation is defined as real it is real in its consequences. It might be added that such definitions are increasingly likely to be nudged, when not shoved, towards the satisfaction of systemic imperatives. In her excellent study of foodbanks, Garthwaite (2016) recounts numerous examples of people struggling to subsist in social worlds that seem to be collapsing around them. Often they experienced feelings of shame and embarrassment when resorting to the use of foodbanks. Glen (aged 52) and Tracey (aged 49) came to the foodbank because of problems with a zero-hour contract (one couple among many experiencing in-work poverty). In Garthwaite's words, they 'looked terrified'. They recounted how they felt on their initial visit:

> *Tracey*: I said to Glen 'Get inside, don't let no one see us', cos obviously we'd never had to go anywhere like that before.
> *Glen*: Ashamed, just felt ashamed.
> *Tracey*: We were just so ashamed we had to go.
> *Garthwaite*: And how did you feel once you got in?
> *Glen*: It was alright cos there were other people in there like us, y'know what I mean? It was like funny when we were going out thinking

> 'Is anybody watching?' all these shopping bags coming out of a church, putting it in the boot of the car. People'd be thinking 'They've got a car and they're going to foodbanks?' The car's our life, I get to work and back on it, but me car's paid for, there's nothing (finance) on it. (Garthwaite, 2016: 145)

Glen and Tracey are here giving voice to the intrusion of felt stigma, a sense of shame compounded by the fear of encountering enacted stigma, and not without reason. Garthwaite (2016: 145–146) writes: 'when people using the foodbank are berated for having cars, tattoos, dogs or iPhones, the very idea that there might have been a life before the foodbank is completely forgotten'.

A number of people had been offered a foodbank voucher but would not accept it, despite being in desperate straits. Maureen, a foodbank volunteer, reflected on a recent experience with a woman who could have got a voucher but had declined to ask for one:

> She came in with this woman and she could have had a voucher as well but she said 'I couldn't get one because I was just too embarrassed about getting it', and it is hard but I said to her 'It's no good being embarrassed if you can't eat.' Y'know, I mean there's no need to be embarrassed because you are entitled to it and your'e in need, and we're happy to do it for you. But at the end of the day you can't stop people feeling that way about it.

Ken Loach captured precisely this mix of desperate need and inhibiting and disabling shame in his film *I Daniel Blake*.

The shame associated with poverty extended far beyond normal foodbank usage. Janice, aged 46 and in the process of appealing against a 'sanction' and subsequent loss of benefits, asked if any toilet rolls were available, confessing that 'I had to send my 11-year old granddaughter to one of our neighbours to ask to borrow a toilet roll – how mortifying is that?' (Garthwaite, 2016: 146). These exchanges are the very stuff of Goffman's dramaturgical analysis, but they also reveal its limitations. Consider Habermas' frame and the sociological task of analysing routine and often ritualistic encounters between foodbank managers or volunteers and clients. These encounters are necessarily, but not always obviously, an amalgam of the communicative action characteristic of the lifeworld and the strategic action characteristic of the system. How is this?

On the face of its staff/client exchanges are typically manifestations of communicative action oriented to consensus; they appear contained within and constrained by lifeworld norms and practices. Staff, many of them volunteers, are present to meet as best they can the often desperate requests of anguished clients. They are a last resort. But this is only part of the story. Distorted communication—signalling the manipulation of clients by staff in line with system imperatives—is doubtless exceptional. Systematically distorted communication—denoting the pursuit of system imperatives notwithstanding staff and clients each conversing in good faith—is by contrast altogether unexceptional. The making of this point requires a move from Goffman's focus on micro-phenomena to meso- and macro-theories (a move of which, it seems, Goffman himself might well have disapproved). Consider the following statement from Garthwaite (2016: 148):

> Even though foodbanks have become so ingrained in daily life in Britain, for the people using them, stigma and shame are all part of walking through the church doors, red voucher in hand. Media portrayals of poverty are fuelling the idea that foodbank users are in some ways to blame for having to ask for a food parcel, creating damaging false distinctions between 'us' and 'them'. This was reflected in the perspectives of the more affluent residents in Stockton-on-Tees. We saw how this can manifest itself in the lived experiences of people using the foodbank, creating a fear so powerful that sometimes it can't be overcome, stopping people from accessing the help they need.

It will be sufficient at this juncture to stress the following:

- stigma (shame) and deviance (blame) are both detectable in these apparently just and solidary exchanges, typically assuming the form of felt stigma and felt deviance, respectively;
- by helping feed the homeless and others caught between a rock and a hard place foodbank staff provide *compensation and cover* for the politics of austerity and its associated welfare cuts, most compellingly represented by the ongoing introduction of Universal Credit;
- these processes of compensating/covering: (a) ameliorate people's suffering; (b) take some of the sting out of government policies ramped up post-2010; and (c) are on the cusp of becoming institutionalised as part and parcel of a neoliberal, neo-Victorian or 'Poor Law' approach to welfare.

Garthwaite highlights the 'risk' of foodbanks being consolidated as an accepted mode of delivery, *as part of the system*, as it already has in other countries.

A Note on 'Territorial Stigma'

It is conspicuously the case that foodbanks carry what has been called a 'territorial stigma': they are places *for* the poor, the marginalised and the desperate, who, it seems, are often blamed for their shame; as Glen and Tracey affirmed they are places not to be seen at or entering. Slater (2018) develops this notion of territorial stigma in his discussion of 'sink estates'. He traces back the etymology of sink estates several centuries, in the process finding that 'it refers to a cesspit for wastewater or sewage – a receptacle that collects and stores effluent ... Wedding 'sink' to a tract of council housing – an act of symbolic violence that turns a receptacle that collects and stores effluent into a *place* that collects and stores the refuse of society – is a journalistic invention, and continues to be (though not exclusively) a journalistic trait' (Slater, 2018: 881). Slater (2018: 877) shows how the derogatory designator 'sink estate', signifying social housing estates that supposedly represent and fuel poverty, family breakdown, worklessness, welfare dependency, antisocial behaviour and personal irresponsibility, has become a 'symbolic frame' used by right-wing journalists and putative think tank 'experts' (notably from Policy Exchange) to justify a raft of neoliberal policies in the era of financial capitalism.

McKenzie (2015) has furnished us with quite another lifeworld-oriented sense of what it is like to live on the kind of estate—in this case in Nottingham—readily and frequently stigmatised as a sink estate. It was an estate that she not only studied but had herself lived on for more than 20 years. Built in the 1970s, she writes, it held no real potential for gentrifiers or property developers. It had a local reputation as a dangerous environment populated by drug dealers and users, single mothers, gangsters and the poor: 'consequently, over several generations, both place and people have been de-valued and stigmatised as valueless' (McKenzie, 2017: 45). She writes of women gathering to socialise and chat in the popular and busy local community centre, and in particular of the role and contribution of a volunteer, 'Sharon'. Sharon turned up every day at 9.15 a.m. after dropping off her children at school. She made drinks, tidied up, talked and listened: her familiar presence helped everyone to relax. She was, in short, 'a lightening rod for local social capital'.

Sharon relied on benefits (adding up to approximately £8500 per annum). She put in a regular 16 hours a week in the community centre but received no remuneration. McKenzie (2017: 46) asked her if she wanted a paid job:

> ... yes, I want to work in the community ... something like a youth worker ... working with the youth on the estate ... although I kind of do that already. That's the kind of job I want ... as long as it pays enough ... enough for the rent and that ... it would be nice to have a car and perhaps a holiday ... but mostly I want to stay in the community.

McKenzie re-interviewed Sharon two years after this exchange, and after the global financial crash of 2008–2009 and the general election of 2010 that saw a Cameron-led coalition government intent on a politics of austerity. The circumstances for both the community centre and for Sharon had changed.

The new Chancellor of the Exchequer, Osborne, opted for £4 billion of welfare cuts. The tropes would become familiar: no longer would the lazy and work-shy be able to live on the backs of hardworking families. 'People who think it is a lifestyle to sit on out-of-work benefits ... that lifestyle choice is going to come to an end. The money will not be there for that lifestyle choice' (cited in McKenzie, 2017: 48). Nor was the money there. The ramifications for Sharon were stark. McKenzie (2017: 48–49) takes up the story and a lengthy quotation is warranted:

> ... I met with Sharon again, and she told me that she had received a letter telling her to go to an appointment at the local benefits agency. During the interview she had been questioned about her availability to work, and she told them she was working, albeit without pay, in the community centre. The adviser asked her whether she thought it was about time she stopped taking from society and gave something back, in the form of paid work. Sharon wanted to work in the local community, but Nottingham City Council had just sent out thousands of 'under threat' redundancy letters to current public sector workers, put a freeze on recruitment, and announced that they had been forced to make public sector spending cuts of £28 million. The benefits agency pushed on with Sharon's case that she needed to get a paid job and contribute to society. Sharon was eventually sanctioned, her benefits cut from £110 per week to £30. Needless to say, she didn't manage well, and admitted defeat, taking the offer of 'help' that the job centre extended to her in putting her forward for a job in a cheese-packing

factory 6 miles away. This meant that Sharon could no longer volunteer at the community centre and had to leave her two children, then aged 7 and 12, alone from 6.30 in the morning to get ready for school themselves. Sharon earned £177 before stoppages for a 30-hour week in the cheese-packing factory, and with the changes in her housing benefit and council tax benefit, she was £9 a week better off financially, although her health very quickly deteriorated through working in a freezing cold environment, and the constant stress of leaving her children alone. After three months Sharon had to quit the job through ill health and depression.

Sharon's experience is far from exceptional. Table 3.2 lists some of the contexts and circumstances in which just a few of the people Garthwaite encountered during her study of foodbanks were sanctioned and were thereby deprived of financial support.

Table 3.2 Contexts for sanctioning people and cutting their benefits

- a man was sanctioned after he missed an appointment because he took his mother to chemotherapy;
- a woman had an interview which lasted longer than she expected, so she was 10 minutes late for her jobcentre appointment and was sanctioned for a month;
- a man was sanctioned for being two minutes late, even though he had turned up 15 minutes early but wasn't allowed to go upstairs to see his adviser until the security guard said so;
- a man missed an appointment after he travelled to Scotland for a family funeral for four members of his family who had been killed in a car crash by a drunk driver. He was sanctioned, even though he rang the jobcentre to tell them he wouldn't be there;
- a woman who went on a health and social care course the jobcentre sent her on was sanctioned for not going to her jobcentre appointment, even though she was on the course the jobcentre had sent her on.

From Garthwaite (2016), cited in Scambler (2018)

Job-centre staff in this account differ from the volunteer workers who feature in foodbanks, as does the nature of the exchanges between each and their clients. It is much easier in the former to see system imperatives and 'open' strategic action for what they are. Encounters between foodbank workers and clients can typically be framed as systematically distorted communication, though distorted communication, or the manipulation of the latter by the former, doubtless occurs. In the context of interaction between job-centre staff and their clients, however, the dominant agenda is unambiguous and many degrees harsher. Distorted communication is the norm, systematically distorted communication the exception. Strategic action sweeps all—or almost all—before it, and communicative action is vanquished. The system rules. This is graphically illustrated by McKenzie's account of Sharon's explicitly humiliating experiences, leading to her shaming (enacted stigma) and blaming (enacted deviance).

So lessons from McKenzie's ethnographic study ally with and build on those from Garthwaite's:

- once again the potency of felt stigma and felt deviance in the lives of Sharon and her neighbours, and their territorial roots in the estate they dwell in, are clear;
- no less apparent are the realities and bite of enacted stigma (shaming) and enacted deviance (blaming);
- the exchanges between women like Sharon and job-centre staff are very different from those between Glen and Tracey and foodbank volunteers in that they are routinely characterised by open strategic rather than communicative action;
- the post-2010 politics of austerity have led not only to the introduction and spread of foodbanks but also to the explicit sabotaging of individual lives and the diminution of community resources and communicative justice and solidarity;
- no Goffman-like, dramaturgical or micro-sociological account of the experiences of Glen and Tracey, or more obviously of Sharon, can do explanatory justice to their situations and circumstances;
- a credible sociology of sham(ing) and blam(ing) must of necessity incorporate a meso-sociology of processes of system-to-lifeworld penetration; and a macro-sociology of system rationalisation or colonisation and of the potential for lifeworld rationalisation or decolonisation (see Table 3.1).

One rider might be added here. What Warr, Taylor, and Williams (2017) call 'poverty stigma' can, as McKenzie affirms, extend to territorial stigma, *but* it can and often is resisted, sometimes with specific reference to territory or space (see the reference in Chapter 2 to project stigma and deviance). This impulse to resist, and the various forms resistance can take, will be revisited later in this text.

AGENCY, CULTURE AND STRUCTURE

To furnish an admittedly ambitious sociology of shaming and blaming along these lines requires clarification on the causal character, relevance and potentials of agency, culture and structure. Each of these concepts will be explicated briefly, drawing on the seminal work of critical realists Bhaskar and Archer as a complement to the critical theory of Habermas.

Agency

It will be apparent that there are seeds of a sociology of shaming and blaming in the situations faced by Glen and Tracey and Sharon and in their responses. They retain agency—as much after all is part of what it is to be human—yet it is deeply embedded, and seemingly constrained far more than enabled, by social structures. Agency, I have argued elsewhere, is *structured but never structurally determined* (Scambler, 2018). Culture too has to be factored in and might be seen as mediating between agency and structure. What does this mean for agency? What too does it mean for sociology? Bourdieu's (1996: 2–3, 5) comment in his book on *Photography* is helpful:

> by its very existence, sociology presupposes the overcoming of the false opposition arbitrarily erected by subjectivists and objectivists. Sociology is only possible as an objective science because of the existence of external relationships which are necessary and independent of individual wills, and, perhaps, unconscious (in the sense that they are not revealed by simple reflection), and which can only be grasped by the indirect route of observation and objective experimentation; in other words, because subjects are not in possession of the meaning of the whole of their behaviour as immediate conscious data, and because their actions always encompass more meanings they know or wish, sociology cannot be a purely introspective science attaining absolute certainty simply by turning to subjective experience, and, by the same token, it can be an objective science of the

objective (and the subjective), i.e. an experimental science, experimentation being, in the words of Bernard, 'the only mediator between the objective and the subjective'.

So helpful is Bourdieu's eloquence here that I will indulge it a little more:

> everything ... takes place as if the shadow cast by objective conditions always extended to consciousness: the intra-conscious reference to objective determinisms which influence practice and always owe some of their effectiveness to the complicity of a subjectivity that bears their stamp and is determined by the hold they exert. Thus the science of objective regularities remains abstract as long as it does not encompass the science of the process of the internalization of objectivity leading to the constitution of those systems of unconscious and durable dispositions that are the class 'habitus' and the 'ethos'; as long as it does not endeavour to establish how the myriad 'small perceptions' of everyday life and the convergent and repeated sanctions of the economic and social universe imperceptibly constitute, from childhood and throughout one's life, by means of constant reminders, this 'unconscious' which becomes paradoxically defined as a practical reference to objective conditions.

This second paragraph has the additional virtue of signalling the continuing salience of class for sociology. Class, I shall maintain, remains pivotal for a sociology of shaming and blaming, notwithstanding the transition in the 1970s from an industrial to a post-industrial or financialised form of capitalism.

What Bourdieu's statements here indicate is that the (lifeworld-oriented) ways in which Glen and Tracey and Sharon define their situations cannot be represented and understood, let alone explained, without reference to the manner of their (system-oriented) structuring. *We are none of us exempt: this is not a function of being disadvantaged, vulnerable or poor.* So the causal power of agency, understood as a mechanism for adaptation and change, cannot be gauged or 'set', not least for sociology, in the absence of an understanding of structure and, next for consideration, culture.

Culture

We are all of us culturally circumscribed, at least initially. Culture via primary and secondary socialisation presents and introduces us to 'our' social worlds by providing frameworks for and modes of understanding and recipes, scripts and predispositions for institutional and social interaction, in Bourdieu's terminology, a 'habitus'. Archer (2014) contends that culture captures 'all intelligibilia', by which she understands any item that has the dispositional capacity of being understood by someone. Intelligibilia, as it were, nestle in a Popperian 'third world' or 'universal archive'. While structural components of society are primarily material, the cultural are largely ideational.

Cultures comprise beliefs, attitudes, value systems, mathematical theorems, scientific theories, novels, poems, paintings, musical scores and so on, each of which sets the scene for and causally influences sociocultural action and its outcomes. A collectivity's ideal interests do not reduce to its material interests. Weber articulated this via his 'switchman simile': 'not ideas, but material and ideal interests, directly govern men's (sic) conduct. Yet very frequently the 'world images' that have been created by 'ideas' have, like switchmen, determined the tracks along which action has been pushed by the dynamics of interest' (cited in Brock, Carrigan, & Scambler, 2017; and see Scambler, 2018). So if ideal interests do not reduce to material interests, they are certainly in their debt. As Archer puts it, structural factors play a significant role in what is adopted from the cultural system and the ends to which it is put.

She goes on to suggest that in areas in which there is a high level of coherence among the ideas, the 'situational logic' is that of *protection*. This is characteristic of early and ancient social formations, in which ideational innovations were generally fought off. In what she calls 'early modernity', the situational logic was one of *correction*, or the reconciling of logical inconsistencies through processes of syncretic refinement. In 'later modernity', by contrast, different materially based interest groups drew selectively on cultural resources to legitimate and further their ends, unleashing a situational logic of *elimination* between their ideas and those of rival or subordinate groups. Archer identifies the present era as 'late modernity' and stresses a situational logic of *opportunity*. The emphasis here is on a group's swift-footed propensity to exploit cultural contingency to its advantage (Archer, 2014).

Structure

Agency and culture alike are structured without being structurally determined. So what is social structure and how, understood via critical realism as a causal mechanism and power, does it express itself in agency and culture? It is axiomatic that at any given historical juncture antecedently existing structures constrain and enable agents, whose culturally informed actions in turn have intended and unintended consequences. It will already be apparent that the experiences, perceptions and actions of Glen and Tracey and of Sharon can be neither described nor explained comprehensively without due consideration of the socially structured and cultural context in which they found themselves, and this independently of their degree of awareness of the salience of this context. As much was alluded to when references were made to the politics of austerity. Warr et al. (2017: 83–84) are eloquent here:

> poverty stigma has proliferated as a result of neoliberal doctrines that have had forceful antisocial effects, if considered against an inclusive interpretation of what constitutes a society. Doctrines promoting the privatisation of state assets, redirection of public spending in favour of market provision, deregulation of economies, shrinking welfare provisions, opposition to organised labour and extending the protection of private ownership are either deliberately or carelessly ruinous of collective welfare. Bauman (2000: 163) noted that these policies have contributed to a 'fading and wilting, falling apart and decomposing of human bonds of communities and partnerships'.

The subtext of this quotation is that there are discernible structural and cultural mechanisms at work in financial capitalism that find their way, often insidiously, into the biographies of many people like Glen, Tracey and Sharon; and, potentially, via the stressors identified by psychologists, under their skins and into their bodies and organs as disease and impairment.

Sociologists who interrogate people's definitions of their situations are obligated to travel—via concepts like Bourdieu's 'habitus' and Archer's 'reflexivity'—from surface phenomena to the beneath-the-surface mechanisms that help deliver and explain them. This is the project of the present text. In Chapter 4, I draw on diverse literatures within and without sociology to postulate a number of meso- or middle-range theories that in my judgement have their contributions to make; and in Chapter 5, I draw on macro-theory to venture a more comprehensive sociology of shaming and blaming that encompasses micro-, meso- and macro-factors. Summarising the discussion at this point, I would stress that:

- for all that people's lifeworld-oriented definitions and accounts of their situations have a validity and authenticity of their own, it is the job of the sociologist to delve deeper to gauge the causal salience of social structural and cultural mechanisms;
- the experience of attending a foodbank or living on a putative 'sink estate' cannot be exclusively accounted for by data deriving from people's subjective accounts (though nor can they accounted for in the absence of such accounts);
- agency and culture are alike in debt to structure while preserving a degree of independence from it;
- another way of articulating the 'independence' of agency and culture is to emphasise the *non-determinism* as well as the necessarily limited brief and purchase of any credible sociology (sociology, like any other genus of mechanisms, cannot wrap things up, not least because of the obdurate survival of free will and the ongoing and sometimes countervailing activity of a multiplicity of social as well as biological and psychological mechanisms);
- it is the responsibility of sociology to push the boundaries of the social and to proffer as comprehensive a description/explanation of shaming and blaming as is within its compass.

References

Archer, M. (2014). The generative mechanisms re-configuring late modernity. In M. Archer (Ed.), *Late modernity* (pp. 92–118). New York: Springer.
Bourdieu, P. (1996). *Photography*. Cambridge: Polity Press.
Brock, T., Carrigan, M., & Scambler, G. (2017). Introduction. In T. Brock, M. Carrigan, & G. Scambler (Eds.), *Structure, culture and agency: Selected papers of Margaret Archer*. London: Routledge.
Cronin, C., & De Greiff, P. (1998). Introduction. In J. Habermas, *The inclusion of the other: Studies in political theory*. Cambridge: Polity Press.
Garthwaite, K. (2016). *Hunger pains: Life inside foodbank Britain*. Bristol: Policy Press.
Habermas, J. (1987). *Theory of communicative action, volume 2: Lifeworld and system: A critique of functionalist reason*. Cambridge: Polity Press.
Habermas, J. (1990). *Moral consciousness and communicative action*. Cambridge: Polity Press.
Habermas, J. (1993). *Justification and application: Remarks on discourse ethics*. Cambridge: Polity Press.

Habermas, J. (1996). *Between facts and norms: Contributions to discourse theory of law and democracy.* Cambridge: Polity Press.
McKenzie, L. (2015). *Getting by: Estates, class and culture.* Bristol: Policy Press.
McKenzie, L. (2017). Valuing and strengthening community. In R. Atkinson, L. McKenzie, & S. Winlow (Eds.), *Building better societies: Promoting social justice in a world falling apart.* Bristol: Policy Press.
Scambler, G. (Ed.). (2001). *Habermas, critical theory and health.* London: Routledge.
Scambler, G. (2018). *Sociology, health and the fractured society: A critical realist account.* London: Routledge.
Slater, T. (2018). The invention of the 'sink estate': Consequential categorisation and the UK housing crisis. *Sociological Review, 66,* 877–897.
Warr, D., Taylor, G., & Williams, R. (2017). Artfully thinking the prosocial. In R. Atkinson, L. Mckenzie, & S. Winlow (Eds.), *Building better societies: Promoting social justice in a world falling apart.* Bristol: Policy Press.

CHAPTER 4

The Neglected Contributions of Middle-Range Social Theory

Abstract This chapter concentrates on the role of middle-range models and theories in helping to explain the emergence and impact of shaming and blaming, of particular interest in Archer's work on reflexivity. The concept of metareflection is introduced, referring to the use of extant social resources in theory and research. Links are explored in this chapter between macro-change, most notably the transition to post-1970s financial capitalism—via meso- or middle-range theories—to the flotsam and jetsom of everyday micro-interaction.

Keywords Middle-range theory · Metareflection · Financial capitalism · Everyday interaction

This chapter is informed by two principal ideas or assertions. The first echoes Merton's (1968) celebration of what he called theories of the 'middle-range' in sociology. His championing of middle-range theory was a response to the gap, some would say chasm, that had opened up in the USA between the macro-sociology of structural-functionalists like Parsons and the micro-sociology of symbolic and other varieties of interactionism (including Goffman's dramaturgy). Merton wanted to fill this gap and sought to do so in his own work on science for example.

The second idea is related. It is summed up by the concept of 'metareflection'. This refers to a positive propensity to pause and take time to reflect on and assess the potential relevance of: (a) existing social

© The Author(s) 2020
G. Scambler, *A Sociology of Shame and Blame*,
https://doi.org/10.1007/978-3-030-23143-9_4

and sociological theory and (b) the vast literature of substantive research. The rationale here is that there is a growing tendency to neglect (a) and (b)—in effect to compress the past—and to give serious consideration only to very recent or 'up to date', 'high impact' contributions. The result of this tendency is the reinvention of any number of tried and tested wheels. Further than this, there is a strong case for perusing (a) and (b) across the full gamut of sociological and allied fields and topics, that is, outside of any specialist field or topic of immediate interest. I have elsewhere tried to show that doing so promises a good return on the investment (Scambler, 2018).

In this chapter, I draw on the theories of Archer on types of reflexivity/reflexive; and on theories of 'ego adjustment' and 'activity reinforcement' developed and deployed elsewhere (Scambler, 2018: 107), and I commend a further middle-range theories salient to shame and blame. For purposes of explication and illustration, the focus is on a sub-category of outsiders, namely those sex workers I have termed 'opportunist migrants' (Scambler, 2007). In the first section, Archer's contribution is set out.

Archer on Types of Reflexivity and Reflexives

Archer argues that personal reflexivity mediates the effects of objective social forms on us: that is, it helps us to understand how structure influences agency. She writes:

> reflexivity performs (this) mediatory role by virtue of the fact that we deliberate about ourselves in relation to the social situations that we confront, certainly fallibly, certainly incompetently and necessarily under our own descriptions, because that is the only way we can know anything. To consider human reflexivity play that role in mediation also means entertaining the fact that we are dealing with two ontologies: the objective pertaining to social emergent properties and the subjective pertaining to agential emergent properties. What is entailed by the above is that subjectivity is not only (a) real, but (b) irreducible, and (c) that it possesses causal efficacy. (Archer, 2007: 42)

What Archer calls the 'internal conversation' denotes the manner in which people 'reflexively' make their way in the world. This inner dialogue about self-in-society and vice versa is what makes most of us 'active' as opposed to 'passive' agents. Being an active agent involves defining, refining and prioritising concerns and constructing and elaborating projects out of them. Agency, as I have argued above, never runs dry. If these projects are successful, constellations of concerns coalesce into a set of practices, and this set of practices constitutes a personal modus vivendi: *concerns lead to projects which lead in turn to practices*. Archer notes, however, that concerns can be ignoble, projects illegal and practices illegitimate. What we do in the course of our internal conversations simultaneously shapes ourselves and contributes to the reshaping of the social world.

Reflexivity, thus understood, does not reduce to one homogeneous mode of deliberation, but is exercised through different modalities. Archer initially discerned three 'dominant modalities'—*communicative, autonomous* and *meta-reflexivity*—but later added a fourth—*fractured* (Archer, 2012). These are summarised in Table 4.1.

Table 4.1 Archer's reflexive modalities

- *Communicative reflexives* are those whose internal conversations require completion and confirmation by others before resulting in a course of action;
- *Autonomous reflexives* are those who sustain self-contained internal conversations, leading directly to action;
- *Meta-reflexives* are those who are critically reflexive about their own internal conversations and critical too about effective action in society;
- *Fractured reflexives* are those whose internal conversations intensify their distress and disorientation rather than leading to purposeful courses of action.

Adapted from Archer (2007, 2012)

Armed with Archer's concepts and modalities or types of reflexivity, it is time now to consider the nature of the—structured but far from structurally determined—lives and embodied experiences of the sub-group migrant sex workers I studied and termed 'opportunists'.

SEX WORK AND SEX WORK STIGMA

As I made clear in the Introduction to this volume, sex work is a heterogeneous occupation and accommodates a wide variety of types of work and worker. There is often said to be a hierarchy of types of work/worker, ranging from street work at one end of the spectrum *up to* elite and exclusive escort and private work (sometimes through 'Madams') at the other, though there can be deep and rebellious resistance to any such ranking on the part of sex workers: street workers are respected in some quarters for their bravery, steadfastness and coping strategies. I have delineated several career trajectories in sex work, summarised in Table 4.2. While this typology is by no means definitive, it does bear testimony to the heterogeneity of sex work.

It is a typology in need of qualification. First, it does not claim to be exhaustive, merely illustrative of the variety of forms of sex work in countries like Britain. Second, it comprises Weberian ideal types: in other words, it neither requires nor suggests that all sex workers fall completely or neatly into one, and only one, of these half dozen career trajectories. Third, and following on, sex workers can and do change careers (e.g. survivors can become workers and vice versa). And fourth, the length of people's careers, like their degree of day-to-day commitment to it, can and does vary.

Common across the sex work industry, notwithstanding its diversity, is the historically long-standing threat of enacted stigma and deviance, with felt stigma and deviance lurking in their shadows. Sex workers have (almost) always been othered as unwelcome, if ubiquitous, outsiders: they are strangers in our midst. Pheterson (1993) has proffered a list of obdurate prostitute/sex worker 'offences' against gendered norms of honour/dishonour which continues to have resonance in financial capitalism. Her list has seven items: having sex with strangers; having sex

Table 4.2 A typology of sex work careers, with examples (Scambler, 2007)

Career	Paradigmatic example
Coerced	Abducted, trafficked
Destined	Family, peers in the trade
Survivors	Drug users, single parents, debtors
Workers	Permanent job
Opportunists	Project financing
Bohemians	Casual, without need

with multiple partners; taking sexual initiative and control and possessing expertise; asking a fee for sex; being committed to satisfying men's lusts and fantasies; being out alone on the streets at night dressed to incite or attract men's desires; being in the company of supposedly drunk or abusive men whom they can either handle (as 'common' or 'vulgar' women) or not handle (as 'victimised' women). The 'whores' or 'bad girls' in Pheterson's representation—calling to mind street rather than indoor workers—contrast strongly with 'Madonnas' or 'good girls' in most cultures. To Pheterson's list might perhaps be added an eighth offence: vector of disease and source of transmission into the respectable (and predominantly heterosexual) community of sexually transmitted infections (STIs), including HIV/AIDS (Scambler, 2007: 1080).

Opportunist Migrants in London

The term 'migrant' is used in a generic sense here to refer to women who travel to London—in my study from Eastern Europe or the former Soviet republics—to work in London as sex workers hiring sexual services through agencies. It will already be clear that the term migrant is inherently problematic (see Agustin, 2006). As we shall see, for all that the 'push' factor of limited or shrinking opportunity in their home countries and the 'pull' factor of high earnings in cities like London are relevant, there remains what Agustin calls 'the conundrum of women's agency'. Why do I refer to these women as 'opportunists'? This is to identify women who come to cities like London with discrete projects in mind, namely, to raise significant funds in a short period of time: for example, to support or become independent of kin, to undertake further or higher education, to rent or buy an apartment or to generally enhance their prospects or well-being. The snowball sample of a dozen women working for one of four central London escort agencies that I interviewed fell into this category of migrant opportunists (Scambler, 2007).

It would of course be wrong to over-extrapolate from conversations with a small non-random sample of 12 women, and my sample is drawn on here only for illustrative purposes. For all my interviewees, sex work was a calculated opportunity to make a lot of money quickly. Six had taken the initiative themselves, two after working in London first in other capacities (as a secretary and a waitress), while the other half knew someone else (usually at home) who had done the same thing and provided introductions. None of the women had been approached initially by an agency.

The four agencies for which the visiting escorts worked cited prices of £150–200 per hour and £500–1000 per night for women's services. The agencies took 33% of this fee, paid in cash to the women by their clients, and the women had to find and pay rental for their flats and cover their living expenses. Monitoring the agencies' websites over a calendar month (May 2005), I found that the services of 78 different women were advertised on 1 May; although the figure was much the same at the end of the month (79), 40% of the initial 78 had by then left the agencies, most, my interviewees informed me, to return home after pre-calculated shifts to raise funds (they had not simply switched agencies or 'gone independent'). This high turnover supports the notion of discrete projects characteristic of opportunistic sex workers.

A prima facie case might be made that these opportunistic migrant sex workers most closely approximate to the idea of 'voluntary adult sex work'. Sex work per se attracts strong moral stances. Two core discourses can be identified in contemporary Britain. The first can be characterised as 'liberal' and is represented by many public health workers. For all that this discourse emerged initially out of a moral panic about HIV/AIDS, it has over time mutated—in part for strategic reasons—towards an advocacy of respectful inclusion. Some now advocate the decriminalisation of (voluntary adult) sex work in Britain. The second discourse is dominated by notions of 'sexual trafficking' and is less tolerant. This discourse conflates migrant sex work with sex trafficking and eschews any reference to voluntary sex work as self-contradictory. Sex workers are here cast either as resolutely immoral or, more often, as victims in need of rescue.

What about the relationship of this particular group of sex workers with their clients? The general literature on sex worker/client relations during encounters allows for several conclusions: (a) clients are as heterogeneous as are sex workers and comprise a significant minority of the adult male population; (b) their motives for visiting sex workers are no less diverse, varying from the satisfying of specific fetishes, to a need to experience intimacy, sexual or otherwise, to wanting company or simply to talk; (c) encounters can, if rarely, generate moments of genuine reciprocity between sex workers and their clients; and (d) sex workers typically work within personal boundaries circumscribing services they will and will not offer, and no less typically 'control' the interaction.

It will be convenient to begin a micro- via meso- towards macro- analysis of the particular set of sex worker/client relations under consideration here with a few comments on aspects of their interaction. Habermas' frame is once more a helpful one. The reference in (d) above to sex workers' protection of self and exercising of control during encounters requires elaboration. Most sex workers stake out their moral territories, holding on to their autonomy via a veto on clients or sexual practices, traditionally kissing but contracting now among some to practices like French kissing, 'oral without'/'coming in the mouth' (OWO/CIM) or anal sex (this is not to underplay the very real risks on those—for escort workers like those in my sample, exceptional—occasions when control is lost (see Barnard's [1993] sobering research on street workers). As far as being in control is concerned, it is ironic that this can be held against sex workers (see Pheterson's notion of the whore stigma), but more often than not with experience comes expertise.

The sex worker/client encounter generally occupies a space that simulates personal, private, intimate space, termed 'smooth space' by Deleuze and Guattari (1987), *but which is actually public, commercialised, regulated or 'striated space'* (Scambler, 2007: 1082). The sex worker typically experiences the encounter as striated space—'within which time ticks so as to mark off units exchanged and money earned'—but works to convince the client that he is experiencing smooth space, within which time 'flows'. The permeability and reversibility of sex worker/client time, however, is considerable (Brewis & Linstead, 1998).

Three additional interactional points are salient. The first is that sex work hinges on a form of emotional labour. As Brewis and Linstead (1998: 230) note, this can be very intense if a client seeks a simulated space, a mock intimacy, where a version of his 'secret self' can gain assurance. This obviously has most applicability to indoor workers like escorts. Second, it is clear that many sex workers develop a 'manufactured identity' for the workplace, often sedimented in ritual practices around time and space. This is both an ego-defence and a business strategy to retain clientele (Sanders, 2005). And finally, as O'Connell Davidson (1998) observes, the reach of the whore stigma is a long one and its grip tenacious. If escorts in the category of London's opportunist migrants can frequently 'pass as normal' and avoid enacted stigma and deviance, felt stigma and deviance are less readily set aside. Only one of the dozen women I interviewed, Leah (aged 23 and divorced), had told her family about her work. Another, Jenny (aged 21 and single), recounted the following episode. Her parents announced an impromptu, unexpected and imminent visit to London to see her. In something of a panic, she arranged to swap flats with a friend for the duration of their stay so as to avoid the territorial stigma—together with its psychological correlates—associated with her workplace.

Deploying Habermas' system/lifeworld and strategic/communicative binaries, this account of the nature of the work of opportunist migrants—accenting calculated and time-bounded projects, learned modes of ego-defence and expert interactional control—suggests a system-like, strategic *manipulation* of clients by sex workers via distorted communication. But does this *prima facie* conclusion stand up to scrutiny? Are clients willing and reflexive contributors to their putative manipulation, to the extent of funding it? More generally, does a meso-orientation require a more refined or revised analysis than that implied so far?

MIDDLE-RANGE THEORY AND OPPORTUNIST MIGRATION

It has been argued that agency and culture are alike structured but never structurally determined. So how might the seemingly deliberative, cost–benefit and actualised or 'made good' 'choices' undertaken by opportunist migrant sex workers be contextualised? I turn first to Archer's explication of reflexivity and her notion of autonomous reflexivity in particular. I characterise the distinctive subset of sex workers in my study as *transitory autonomous reflexives*. Table 4.3 presents an ideal type of the transitory autonomous reflexive. It presents, as a subset of Archer's autonomous reflexives, a portrait of young women who, unsatisfied with the lot accorded to them by what Archer would call their 'natal involuntary placement' in their home societies, weigh up the options available and resolve to take decisive action to improve their prospects, typically with specific objectives or projects and a timescale in view. Doubtless as a function of biological and psychological as well as social mechanisms, they have the wherewithal to hold themselves together and a narrative for self and maybe others to underpin it. Importantly, it should not be inferred that the qualities that make for entry to the sex industry are spread evenly across all the women's status- and role-sets.

Table 4.3 Attributes of the transitory autonomous reflexive

Internal locus of control

A sense of active engagement with the social world and that agency can/will make a difference

Risk-takers

A willingness to take what to others might seem to be a 'gamble' in order to adopt and realise specific short- or medium-term goals

Status and role differentiation

A capacity to compartmentalise aspects of the dialectic between agency and life course, for example by delineating and 'separating out' the status (position) and role (expectations attaching to that position) of 'temporary sex worker' from the totality of status- and role-sets.

Facility to plan

A commitment to planning—conceiving, preparing and following—a specific course of action.

Project orientation

A propensity to focus in on an immediate project as a worthwhile investment of time, energy.

Strong will and stamina

A calculated willingness to see a project through to completion—'stickability'—even in the context of ups and downs and against apparently long odds.

Project stigma and deviance

An implicit resolve to avoid/not submit to enacted or felt stigma and/or deviance.

Ego adjustment

A propensity to incorporate projects into a viable narrative for self and others.

The notion of ego adjustment is here incorporated in the ideal type of the transitory autonomous reflexive, but it calls for some elaboration. It stands on its own feet as a middle-range model asserting that people's definitions of self, situation and orientation to society as well as to social and personal change are typically embedded in rationalisations—in the form of narratives—*that fit their circumstances and are appropriate to their desires*. These rationalisations also afford a moral warranty. In other words, they serve to justify people's definitions and actions.

Another relevant and kindred middle-range theory is that of 'activity reinforcement'. This maintains that what becomes familiar through repetition more insistently structures agency and is more causally efficacious than is commonly thought. This points to a tendency for the repetition-cum-familiarity associated with status and role-set occupancy—or in the case of migrant opportunist sex workers their specific status and role *as sex workers*—to translate into a behavioural predictability beyond the conscious reach of ego adjustment, even if this is time-limited.

A third model or theory of the middle-range concerns culture, and might be regarded as at one with Archer's situational logic of opportunity. I shall refer to it under the rubric of 'cultural facilitation'. Cultures and subcultures can be enabling or constraining, can *facilitate* some courses of action and provide hoops and obstacles for others. In the present context, it is clear that migrant opportunist sex workers opened a window of opportunity when they distanced themselves, literally, from their 'home' families, communities and circumstances: they gained a degree of anonymity. But beyond this helpful traversing of borders and cultural distancing, these transitory autonomous reflexives brought with them from Eastern Europe and the former Soviet bloc a degree of atheistic immunity from the internalisations of Christian (and other religious) enmity towards and sanctions on sexual activity and sex work. They did not have to face the personal torments, guilt and angst common among indigenous workers. This released them—without penalties of conscience—both to work and to make available services outside of and beyond standard London markets (Scambler, 2007).

Apposite at this juncture is a reflection or two on the macro-sociological underpinning of these meso-sociological inputs, albeit this is properly the subject matter of the next chapter. Metareflection, or the mining of sociology's extant theoretical and substantive literature *across the full or intersectional gamut of domains*, is compelling. In relation to the opportunist migrant sex workers featured in this chapter, the following points might be made:

- any exercise of agency on the part of the sex workers travelling to London from Eastern Europe and the former Soviet states to raise monies to realise projects must be set in the context not only of the micro- and meso-theories adumbrated so far, but against the structural background of declining job prospects in the formal economy, and even the decline of basic schooling.
- The 'new inequality' in post-communist Eastern Europe can be traced to a resurgence of class relations aided, abetted and exported from the post-industrial, post-welfare-statist or financialised capitalism of the West. The strategic action of the sex industry's own *illicit* and increasingly globalised cabal of 'impressarios' operating in the informal economy mimics and caricatures more formal relations of class (Agathangelou, 2004).
- Rates of profit and exploitation can be very high. From my study, Carla, aged 20 and living with an alcoholic father in Riga, said she could earn in two hours of escort work in London as much as she could earn in a month 'at home'; but her stint of two weeks still offered a considerable return for her agency (and she was one of 23 on their books). Carla's project was to earn sufficient to get a flat of her own and to commence studying; she had spent two weeks as an escort in Zurich six months before coming to London (Scambler, 2007: 1088).
- Class relations do not only afford a recruitment pool for sex work entrepreneurs and the potential to commodify and exploit women's bodies, they also shape cultural change. As Sklair (2000) argues, financial capitalism has spawned—if not in any sense 'determined'—a 'culture-ideology of consumption' consonant with its requirements.
- Financial capitalism has been accompanied by a (postmodern or) cultural relativism that has seen what Lyotard (1984) terms *grand*—unified, universal—narratives displaced by multiple *petit*— fragmented or relativised—narratives. This has a special relevance for sex work in an era of 'plastic sexuality', whereby sex has been separated from procreation (Giddens, 1992); hierarchical heterosexuality has lost some of its regulatory power, as have extra- or

non-'couplehood' sexual relations (Gross, 2005); and eroticism has now been 'emancipated' not only from sex but also from *love* (Bauman, 1998).
- The 'command relations' of the state remain semi-detached from Britain's sex industry, leaving sex work largely invisible and in the hands of its entrepreneurs/exploiters. There is evidence that in recent times the political elite at the apex of apparatus of the state has been more accommodating to the harsher sexual trafficking discourse than to the more liberal public health discourse. According to the latter, all opportunist migrant sex workers are 'Natashas' in urgent need of rescue (though in practice to rescue is to eject from the UK). It needs to be stressed that investigations into sexual trafficking—which is of course defended by nobody—have shown it to be exceptional in the UK.
- Gender relations long preceded those of class and command, neither of which are intrinsically or necessarily gendered for all that they have been comprehensively 'masculinised'. Women's restricted options and opportunities and lower incomes, together with the core properties of the whore stigma, have alike survived in contemporary postmodern or relativised culture. Nor are the personally troubling predicaments of women in Eastern Europe and the old Soviet countries coincidental: for many it represents but one aspect of a ubiquitous 'feminisation of poverty'. And critically, it must be added that men in pre-capitalist as well as in liberal, industrial and post-industrial capitalism have sustained institutional means for satisfying their desires (Ringdal, 2004). Pre-existing institutions were simply, if innovatively, re-cast with the advent of capitalism after the manner of the class relations of the formal economy.
- Ethnic relations too were typically established long before capitalism. Like those of gender, they are not strictly required for capitalism, although *contemporary* forms of neo-colonialism can only be structurally elaborated in terms of relations of class and command. As far as the sex workers referenced in this chapter are concerned, Agathangelou (2004) has perspicuously described them as 'white but not quite'. In deploying this phrase, she announces two themes. First, ethnic relations play a significant role in facilitating and legitimating the exploitative and oppressive aspects of London's sex industry; and second, through the medium of racial stereotyping, they complement the erotic with the exotic, feeding clients'

fantasies and 'demands for difference' and enhancing profits in the process (Scambler, 2007: 1090).
• Theorising stigma relations requires going beyond Goffman to address agency and culture against the backcloth of structure. The women in my small study were responsive to the notion of the whore stigma, most notably around what Goffman called the 'management of information', and were thus vulnerable to felt stigma and deviance. Day and Ward (2004: 166), who conducted an impressive 15 year prospective study of 130 women across all facets of the industry, might be quoted here:

> In brief, sex workers came into the industry concerned about a blemish on their characters; they shared views that were common inside and outside prostitution about this 'whore stigma'. After a short time, however, women represented stigma in largely social and structural terms, emphasising how this 'whore stigma' was produced and reproduced through policy, law, gender relations and the organisation of work. The 'whore stigma' was thereby credited largely to the external world. Later still, women were often concerned once more about a blemish on their own characters albeit one caused by social oppression. More specifically, they felt that the stigma had affected their lives and they spoke especially about their mental well-being and life chances.

These latter paragraphs are a prolegomenon for the subject matter of the next chapter. Having shown via a protracted discussion of one aspect of the sex industry, how the micro-sociology of Goffman requires deepening and contextualising by the formation and refining of meso-sociology, it is time now to focus on the salience of macro-social structures for shaming and blaming.

References

Agathangelou, A. (2004). *The global political economy of sex: Desire, violence and insecurity in Mediterranean nation states*. London: Palgrave.
Agustin, L. (2006). The conundrum of women's agency: Migration and the sex industry. In R. Campbell & M. O'Neill (Eds.), *Sex work now* (pp. 116–140). Cullompton: Willan Press.
Archer, M. (2007). *Making our way in the world*. Cambridge: Cambridge University Press.
Archer, M. (2012). *The reflexive imperative*. Cambridge: Cambridge University Press.

Barnard, M. (1993). Violence and vulnerability: Conditions of work for street-working prostitutes. *Sociology of Health and Illness, 15,* 683–705.

Bauman, Z. (1998). On postmodern uses of sex. *Theory, Culture and Society, 15,* 19–33.

Brewis, J., & Linstead, S. (1998). Time after time: The temporal organisation of red-collar work. *Time and Society, 7,* 223–248.

Day, S., & Ward, H. (2004). Approaching health through the prism of stigma: Research in seven European countries. In S. Day & H. Ward (Eds.), *Sex work, mobility and health in Europe* (pp. 139–159). London: Routledge & Kegan Paul.

Deleuze, G., & Guattari, F. (1987). *A thousand plateaus: Capitalism and schizophrenia.* Minneapolis: University of Minneapolis Press.

Giddens, A. (1992). *The transformation of intimacy: Sexuality, love and eroticism.* Cambridge: Polity Press.

Gross, N. (2005). The de-traditionalisation of intimacy reconsidered. *Sociological Theory, 23,* 286–311.

Lyotard, J.-F. (1984). *The postmodern condition.* Manchester: Manchester University Press.

Merton, T. (1968). *Social theory and social structure.* New York: Free Press.

O'Connell Davidson, J. (1998). *Prostitution, power and freedom.* Cambridge: Polity Press.

Pheterson, G. (1993). The whore stigma: Female dishonour and male unworthiness. *Social Text, 37,* 39–54.

Ringdal, N. (2004). *Love for sale: A global history of prostitution.* London: Atlantic Books.

Sanders, T. (2005). 'It's just acting': Sex workers' strategies for capitalising on sexuality. *Gender, Work and Organisation, 12,* 319–342.

Scambler, G. (2007). Sex work stigma: Opportunist migrants in London. *Sociology, 41,* 1079–1096.

Scambler, G. (2018). *Sociology, health and the fractured society: A critical realist account.* London: Routledge.

Sklair, L. (2000). *The transnational capitalist class.* Oxford: Blackwell.

CHAPTER 5

The Salience of Macro-Sociology

Abstract This chapter builds on the earlier introduction to critical realism to note the importance of causal 'tendencies' and interdisciplinarity in the study of open societies. The chapter also extends the conceptualisations of stigma and deviance of earlier discussions. It moves on to discern a 'weaponising of stigma' in the form of 'abjection'. This weaponising, it is argued, represents an unambiguous political strategy in financial capitalism and is routinely deployed against vulnerable segments of the population.

Keywords Open society · Weaponising stigma · Abjection · Politics of appending blame to shame

In the concluding section of Chapter 4, it was suggested that excursions into macro-sociology are necessary for a comprehensive sociology of shaming and blaming. Sex work encounters have their main or tap roots in social structures and social change. It is the brief of this chapter to consolidate and develop this argument. This will be accomplished by reference to two particular sub-populations, those with long terms illnesses and/or disabilities and migrants and refugees. First, however, it is important to establish the parameters of post-1970s financial capitalism.

Social Order and Social Dynamics: Contemporary Financial Capitalism

The present always draws in the past and the future: to describe it is to accommodate both the past that preceded, informed and still nestles within it, and the future imaginaries that define present-day aspirations and projects. It will be expedient here to say something of financial capitalism's genesis. During liberal and on into early Fordist capitalism, from 1820 to World War I, the market provided 'system integration' by coordinating the production and distribution of material goods, and 'social integration' via the provision of norms, values and identities that reinforced people's economic motivation. Convictions about equal opportunity, upward mobility, the work ethic and that talent plus endeavour would be recognised and rewarded were more commonplace than in subsequent eras. As system and social integration were indebted to the market, liberal capitalism was prone to crisis. This was to change with the switch through late Fordist to welfare capitalism, dating approximately from World War I to the early 1970s.

I draw here on the summary account in Scambler (2018a). Post-World War II welfare capitalism diverged markedly from its predecessor. It was corporate rather than market dominated. More specifically, transnational corporations came to monopolise production, set prices and manipulate demand, in the process nullifying any putative benefits deriving from 'free' market competition, price reduction, and so on. It was an era characterised too by much more state intervention, in part a response to liberal capitalism's failure to deliver system and social integration. The state progressively underwrote basic but unprofitable goods and services; maintained the infrastructure; subsidised education and training for workers; provided social insurance cover for the unemployed, people with disabilities and the retired; and addressed and attempted to mitigate the ecological by-products of capitalism. In the process of these interventions on the part of the state, potential crises were displaced from economy to state, hence Habermas' (1975) stress in the mid-1970s on likely crises of (state) legitimacy.

The transition to financial capitalism was signalled in the 1970s by the American abrogation of Bretton Woods and the rise of the Eurodollar, which freed up money capital from national regulation by central banks. The international recession sucked banks further and deeper into the global arena. This had serious consequences: the emergence and consolidation of transnational finance as internationalised banks established closer relations with transnational corporations; and the resurgence of money capital in the lead capitalist economies. References to processes of 'financialisation' became increasingly familiar, capturing not only the phenomena of de-regulation and internationalisation, but also a shift in the distribution of profits from productive to money capital (accompanied by an increase in the external financing of industry). The financial domain came to penetrate the very core of industrial corporations. Industrial capital more and more resembled financial capital. In the financial sector itself, de-regulation precipitated capital centralisation in banks with global reach whose activities encompassed both financial production and speculation in derivatives, even as institutional investors controlling capitalised deferred wages became centres of allocative as well as strategic power (Carroll, 2008). Then came the global financial crisis of 2008–2009.

Articulated in Habermasian terms, these developments heralded a significant change in system rationalisation and in system/lifeworld relations. I have argued that pivotal to this change is a new, or heavily revised, *class/command dynamic* (Scambler, 2018a, 2018b). With the transition to financial capitalism came some quite fundamental changes to the distribution of types of work and to class as its core structure or set of relations. These changes in 'types of work' are represented in Table 5.1, which is adapted from analyses by Bukodi and Goldthorpe (2019: 36), who deploy a well-established proxy for class, NS-SEC. Several points must be made before the notion of the class/command dynamic is defined and elucidated. First, it is in my view perfectly appropriate to use an instrument like NS-SEC to appraise the degree of absolute and relative social mobility that has occurred in post-war Britain. Second, it does *not* follow from this that NS-SEC, derived from the work of Weber rather than Marx, and devised specifically for social mobility studies, is a satisfactory proxy for class considered as a social structure or set of relations, that is, in critical realist terms, a *really existing* generative or causal mechanism. Third, like virtually all proxies for class used for the purposes of quantitative sociological research, NS-SEC 'absents' the (really existing and most causally efficacious) class grouping *that trumps all others* and that informs my concept of financial capitalism's novel class/command dynamic (Scambler & Scambler, 2015). What goes missing in the likes of NS-SEC is the class grouping that, adapting Clement and Myles (1997), I have called the 'capitalist executive'.

Table 5.1 The changing class distribution

NS-SEC classification, with examples:
Class 1: Higher managers and professionals
(e.g. general managers in large companies and organisations, higher-grade civil servants and local government officials, architects, lawyers, medical practitioners, professional engineers, scientists, university teachers)
Class 2: Lower managers and professionals
(e.g. general managers in small companies and organisations, site managers, office managers, workshop managers, lower-grade civil servants and local government officers, librarians, nurses, physiotherapists, school teachers, social workers, surveyors)
Class 3: Ancillary professional and administrative
(e.g. computer maintenance staff, draughtspersons, library assistants, nursery nurses, paramedical staff, cashiers, clerical workers, data processing operators, personal assistants, secretaries)
Class 4: Small employers and own account workers
(e.g. garage proprietors, builders, café proprietors, craftsmen, market traders, publicans, shopkeepers)
Class 5: Lower supervisory and technical occupations
(e.g. foremen, and site and works supervisors, auto-engineers, heating engineers, instrument technicians, laboratory technicians, printers, tool- and pattern-makers, TV and video engineers)
Class 6: Semi-routine occupations
(e.g. care assistants, caretakers and housekeepers, chefs and cooks, chemical process workers, crane drivers, factory machinists, fitters, postal workers, receptionists, sales assistants, store controllers and despatchers, traffic wardens)
Class 7: Routine occupations
(e.g. bus and van drivers, construction site and other labourers, craftsmen's mates, food process workers, counter and bar staff, house and office cleaners, kitchen assistants, packers and fillers, porters and attendants, refuse collectors, warehouse workers).

Bukodi and Goldthorpe's offer the following summary statements. As far as men are concerned, they write:

> In 1951 the wage-earning working class, as represented by NS-SEC Classes 6 and 7, was predominant, accounting for well over half the active male population. In contrast, the managerial and professional salariat, as represented by Classes 1 and 2, accounted for little more than a tenth. But over the period covered the working class contracts and the salariat expands, and especially rapidly between 1951 and 1991. Thus, by 2011 the working class is reduced to less than a third of the active male population while the salariat comprises around two-fifths. The three intermediate classes, NS-SEC Classes 3, 4 and 5, remain more stable in size, although some slight decline is indicated in the proportion of men in Class 3, that of employees in ancillary professional and administrative occupations.

And for women:

> In the case of women, the distributions change for the most part in the same way as with men, even if somewhat more slowly, and in particular the increase in the proportion in the higher-level managerial and professional positions of NS-SEC Class 1 is less marked. The one major difference from men comes with NS-SEC Class 3 which between 1951 and 1971 expanded so as to account for over a third of the active female population but then contracted so as to account for only a quarter by 2011—a reflection chiefly of the rise and fall of the office secretary and typist.

The table below records the class, NS-SEC, distributions (%) of economically active populations, 1951–2011:

Class				
Men				
1	4	10	15	18
2	7	15	20	22
3+4+5	10 – 10 – 14	8 – 10 – 12	8 – 10 – 12	7 – 13 – 10
6+7	55	45	35	30
	1951	1971	1991	2011

Women				
1	2	4	7	8
2	6	10	20	22
3+4+5	30 – 6 – 6	36 – 4 – 4	30 – 4 – 4	25 – 6 – 4
6+7	50	42	35	35
	1951	1971	1991	2011

Such, in short, has been the shift from an industrial to a post-industrial social formation.

My adaptation of the capitalist executive is encapsulated in Table 5.2 (for further details, see Scambler, 2018a, 2018b). Its hard core of aptly named 'capital monopolists' comprise a mere fraction—maybe 0.1% of the population—as opposed to the Occupy Movement's now notorious *1%*. They are heavily globalised and together constitute the prime class driver for social order and social dynamics. Complementing the intra-class alliances and 'class habitus' that characterise the capitalist executive as a whole, there necessarily exist paid-off co-optees from all classes.

Table 5.2 The capitalist executive

The capitalist executive consists of largely transnational group of 'detached', 'post-national' or 'nomadic' owners of significant capital. They might be further delineated as follows:

Capital monopolists: a hard core of heavy capital owners who are 'players', that is, who privilege—whose life is—capital accumulation above all else.

Capital auxiliaries: a soft(er) auxiliary grouping of heavy capital owners who are 'non-players', that is, whose lives are not dedicated to capital accumulation but facilitate and benefit from it.

Capital sleepers: insiders constituting a tier of higher management, light capital owners whose support of 'player' activity affords a kind of infrastructure.

> I have maintained that together the capital monopolists and the state's power elite comprise a 'governing oligarchy' or plutocracy disguised as a form of parliamentary democracy.
>
> Adapted from Scambler (2018a).

'Men of wealth buy men of power', observed US historian Landes (1998), presciently (picking up on the—white—patriarchal history of the Occident). The capital monopolists (the purchasers) and the power elite that heads the apparatus of the state (the purchased) add up to a 'governing oligarchy' or, as some prefer, plutocracy. In such a manner are we now ruled. It is not the increasingly heterogeneous assembly of interchangeable personnel involved that matters (see Davis, 2018), but rather the economic structures and relations of class and the state structures and relations of command that they 'surf' and that contribute most effectively to Habermas' system colonisation of the lifeworld.

The novelty of the class/command dynamic of financial capitalism is that capitalist monopolists can now buy much more power from agents of the state to make and implement policy in their interests, that is, favouring the accumulation of further capital, than hitherto. Objectively, class relations have ramped up their salience in financial capitalism, *even as subjectively they have lost salience for identity formation, for people's sense of who they are and what they are about*. The class/command dynamic, thus defined, is for me the principal causal contributor to system rationalisation and the colonisation of the lifeworld. It provides, as I seek to show in this and the next chapter, a key theme for sociology of shaming and blaming.

Other of its companion changes in financial capitalism include:

- *The ubiquity of neoliberal ideology*: 'neoliberalism' is a contested umbrella term for a worldview that presently traverses the globe, granting a more or less free warranty to capital executives and their allies to maximise returns on their capital.
- *The new generalised potency of owning and inheriting capital*: the accumulation of ever more obscene amounts of capital by capital monopolists is undeniable, but, as Piketty (2014) painstakingly

documents, inheriting capital is becoming a prerequisite for material security, in terms of both home ownership and the financing of a secure, healthy and comfortable quality of life.
- *The new inequality*: during financial capitalism wealth in general and income in particular have been taken from: (a) the already precariously placed 'have-nots' and (b) the 'squeezed middle', and donated to (c) the top 0.1% and (d) dispersed to the remainder of the top 10% plus their allies from the non-squeezed or upper reaches of the middle class (Clark & Heath, 2014).
- *The new culture*: the culture of financial capitalism has witnessed both the emergence and preponderance of a more extreme form of individualism and its postmodernisation or relativisation, one consequence of which has been a pulling of the rug beneath rationally compelling lifeworld-generated narratives for utopian rather than dystopian alternate social institutions and societies. The current phase of 'post-truth' or 'anything goes': (a) provides implicit protection for neoliberal ideology by denying worldviews, (b) encourages irrational quests for certainty and 'fundamentalisms' in ambiguous times, and ultimately (c) represents a new form of neo-conservatism (Habermas, 1989).
- *'Higher immorality'*: financial capitalism's hyper-individualism has not only been associated with a generalised, self-centred decline in empathy for and compassion toward others (a 'lower immortality'), but, the other side of the same coin, by what C. W. Mills (1956) called a 'higher immorality' on the part of capital monopolists and the capitalist executive together with their inter-class allies and co-optees. The latter have no compunction now in maximising the return on their capital, in 'making money' (I have characterised them elsewhere as 'focused autonomous reflexives' [Scambler, 2012, 2018a]). They are, in Habermas' terminology, consumed by forms of strategic action oriented to their own enrichment.

Brexit

One way of adding flesh to this somewhat arcane and skeletal characterisation of financial capitalism's structural and cultural parameters is via a brief digression on Brexit. Brexit, like the election of Trump in the USA, can be taken as a symptom of what I have called a 'fractured society'. On 23 June 2016, in the face of urgent exhortations to the contrary by

Prime Minister Cameron, a narrow majority of the British (51.9%) voted in a referendum in favour of quitting the European Union (EU). Why? Castells (2019: 57–68) argues that the campaigns for and against continuing membership—both of which erred on the side of negativity— were not decisive: in fact, the negativity occasioned widespread public criticism. Castells contends that the seeds of the 'leave' majority were sown some considerable time before the referendum: 'people categorize and assess the information that they receive based on their pre-existing convictions, rooted in the emotions that they feel: electoral deliberation is secondary'. Moreover 'British exceptionalism' had deep historical, geographical and institutional roots. Britain might have had an eye on European markets, but it had long been resistant to any form of political integration and relations and negotiations had always proved tense.

Prior to the referendum in 2016, the three major political parties were all pro-European, save for a minority Eurosceptic faction in the Conservative Party. But according to Castells a significant turning point was reached when public dissatisfaction with government policies, Conservative and Labour, became linked to Britain's subordination to the EU in the wake of financial globalisation, industrial delocalisation and rising immigration ('to put it another way, things changed when the debate broadened out to include the general public at large, and not just the political classes' (Castells, 2019: 59). The emergence of the ultra-right-wing United Kingdom Independence Party (UKIP) had tapped into public dissatisfaction and posed a growing electoral threat to the Conservatives. Cameron sought to channel public disaffection by promising a referendum on the EU in the run-up to the 2015 general election. It worked, UKIP's appeal was blunted and the Conservatives were returned with an outright majority.

'Take Back Control' was at the core of the Brexiteers' campaign. This reassertion of national sovereignty, Castells suggests, was less a nostalgic reference to past 'glories' of British imperialism than a defensive reflex focused around 'the protection of their right to live in their country, undisturbed'. Key here was a rejection of Europeans citizens' right to free migration. As alluded to in the Introduction, since 2004, and as a result of measures taken by Blair to open borders to European migration, the numbers of migrants from Eastern Europe had risen significantly. In the context of the neoliberal politics of austerity and associated budget cuts following the 2008–2009 global financial crisis, this particular source of EU migration became a cipher for the invasion of people's lifeworlds by globalisation in all its nefarious guises and disguises. Castells (2019: 61) writes:

> clearly, then, the explicit reasons that people rallied around the idea of Brexit were greater control of the country's borders and a rejection of immigration. In 2015, support for leaving the European Union was 40 percentage points higher amongst those who felt that immigration was too high than it was amongst people who had no objection to immigrants. What was really being expressed through opposition to immigration and the EU was in fact the profound class and cultural divide that defines British society, and the Western societies more generally. The local objected to the global using the only tool at hand: the border. Markets and capital are allowed to cross it by all means, provided that they don't bring people and cultures with them. This basic social division becomes patently clear when we look at exactly who voted for Brexit.

Those who voted disproportionately in favour of Brexit were people aged over 65; people with lower levels of professional qualifications or education; the industrial working class; white people; and residents of cities and regions most distanced from metropolitan centres and Greater London, most notably in the north of England. Of course, such demi-regs require qualification (e.g. there is a larger population of people 65+ than of those aged under 30, and the latter were also less likely to vote), and they can in any case only yield explanatory clues. Castells asks whether the pro-Brexit vote might be regarded as 'reactionary'. His response is cautiously affirmative. It was in his view a reaction against 'the multidimensional and uncontrolled change that is shaking our world, from automation to cultural hybridisation'. It was a reaction against the gathering pace of the system rationalisation and colonisation of the lifeworld. It was also an appeal to the command relations of the state to reign in and compensate for those of class, and to the extent that this was a desperate and forlorn appeal in the continuing absence of a crisis of state legitimation blame was projected onto the EU. Brexit, for Castells, was less a traditional class vote than a vote by those who 'felt left behind', the marginalised.

The principal qualification that I would add to Castells' helpful analysis is that while 'traditional'—that is, Fordist, industrial, welfare statist—class alignments, commitments and behaviours have to some extent become hidden in the mists of cultural change in post-Fordist, post-welfare statist financial capitalism, class as structure and relation now bites deeper than before. Objective class relations have grown stronger even as: (a) they now have 'cultural cover', and (b) subjectively, class has diminished its causal input into identity formation as well as 'alignments, commitments and behaviours'. The class/command dynamic rules, *literally*.

But how does this brief macro-sociology of financial capitalism and the illustratory reference to Brexit fuel a sociology of shaming and blaming that journeys further down the meso- to micro-line in open or concealed (distorted or systematically distorted) communication? It is a question addressed here in terms of the literatures on long term or disabling illness and the experiences of migrants and refugees.

Long Term and/or Disabling Illness

The interactionist or Goffmanesque orientation to what was in the 1970s and 1980s called chronic illness—the 'personal tragedy' approach—was introduced earlier. To recap, its focus was on how people who somehow or other attracted or came by a state-sanctioned and therefore culturally authoritative medical diagnosis or label *adapted and coped* with this tragic intrusion into their lifeworlds. Scant attention was paid to the labellers as opposed to the labelled. This personal tragedy or *social deviance* paradigm entrenched in medical sociology was appropriately challenged by disability theorists and activists, who emphasised the oppressive character both of such processes of labelling, together with their imputations of deviance, and of the structural and cultural properties—lack of institutional accessibility and inclusion—that underpinned it.

Disability theorists rejected as prejudicial any notion of the long term sick and disabled as socially deviant individuals: the normal/deviant dualism was judged altogether inappropriate for the study of disability or disabled people. Thomas (2007: 4) summarises as follows:

> ... sociologists in disability studies use a 'social oppression' paradigm: to be disabled, or to be discursively constructed as 'disabled', is to be subject to social oppression. 'Disablism' functions alongside sexism, racism, ageism and homophobia in society. Medical sociologists, I argue, theorise chronic illness and disability through the 'social deviance' lens, and have done so in different theoretical guises for many years. Ideas about social deviance

have infused medical sociologists' analyses of two main themes: societal responses to people designated chronically ill or disabled, and the social experience of living with stigmatised body states. Theoretical diversity is evident in both the oppression and social deviance paradigms.

Thomas later suggested that disability studies, or the sociology of disability, has edged towards a new branch of equality and diversity studies.

The Thatcher years (1979–1991) marked an enthusiastic consolidation of the new era of financial capitalism and also saw a closing down of avenues and options for people with disabilities (though they also bore witness to an equally new oppositional consciousness and embryonic movement. The post-Thatcher/Major years of the New Labour regime (1997–2010) steadied the ship; but the more recent premierships of Cameron (with Clegg and the Liberal Democrats in tow) and his hapless successor May, and their enduring politics of austerity and welfare cuts, have since left people with disabilities severely disadvantaged. I shall argued that it is impossible to adequately understand or explain the neoliberalism that has characterised all UK governments from 1979 without referring back to financial capitalism's class/command dynamic and its companion cultural shifts; and that it is no more possible to account for the merciless political discrimination (disablism) against so many people with disabilities, right down to their intolerable humiliation at the doors of DWP offices and foodbanks, in the absence of such a macro-sociological perspective.

It was the New Labour government that launched the work capability assessment (WCA) in 2008, explicitly to cut the benefits bill. This involved redefining disability and the retesting of people who had been in receipt of the old incapacity benefit. The 'model' on which the test to see if people were eligible for the Employment and Support Allowance (ESA) was based predicted that 23% of them would fail and be found fit for work. That the early tests were flawed was confirmed when people with terminal cancer were deemed fit for work, but WCA was rolled out anyway in 2010. The Cameron government then contracted out the retesting programme to ATOS, and by 2012 hundreds of thousands of people were heading to tribunals to appeal their fit-to-work assessments (on average 40% of those refused benefit go to tribunal, of whom 40% are subsequently granted the benefit). In 2013, it was revealed that 1200 people had died after being informed that they should begin preparations to go to work. ATOS, hitherto a low-profile French IT firm, came under sustained attack and eventually left the contract (which had been worth £80 million per annum). Astonishingly, ATOS was then awarded a separate contract to perform another disability assessment—Personal Independence Payments (PIP)—which was designed to deliver savings of 20%. This was launched in 2013. Meanwhile, Maximus took over from ATOS to test for eligibility for ESA. There was to be no amelioration of policy when May took over from Cameron in 2015 following the referendum majority for Brexit (Scambler, 2018b).

The upshot of this tranche of legal changes, amounting in combination to a significant attack on the standards of living and quality of life of people with disabilities, has been inordinate hardship, culminating only too often in deteriorating health and well-being and none too rarely in suicide. Changes that had their genesis in systemic and class-driven shifts in governance and economic, social and health policy have insinuated their way into the private sector lifeworlds of people with disabilities and driven many to despair and worse.

Migrants and Refugees

In the Introduction to this book, the rapidly increasing scale of transnational migration into the twenty-first century was emphasised and a special note made of the impact of this on the EU and Britain. Little was said of the refugee 'community' in Britain, of this disparate body of 'strangers in our midst'. I focus here on refugees. Table 5.3 derives from the Refugee Council's summary of British government statistics up to the end of 2018. The statistics coalesce around 'top 20 facts about refugees and people seeking asylum'. No apology is made for either its inclusion or its comprehensiveness. The statistics are tortuously eloquent. They testify to a reluctance to accommodate displaced persons epitomised recently by the British Home Secretary Sajid Javid:

> if you had survived years of conflict in Syria or South Sudan, seen multiple family members perish, made a desperate, life-threatening dash for Europe that ended in a camp in northern France, but had a father or a sister in the UK, would you risk your life to try and join them? Our home secretary, Sajid Javid, is certain he would not. At least, that was the implication of the question he posed on a visit to Dover last week. 'If you are a genuine asylum seeker why have you not sought asylum in the first safe country that you arrived in', he asked. (Observer Editorial, 2019).

Table 5.3 Top 20 facts about refugees and asylum seekers

The world is in the grip of one of the worst forced displacement crises ever.

Around the globe, the equivalent of the whole British population has had to leave their homes, millions of them fleeing their country of origin to become refugees.

It is poor, not rich, western countries who look after the vast majority of the world's refugees.

The UN's Refugee Agency estimates that 85% of the world's refugees are sheltered by developing countries.

Given the world is facing the greatest refugee crisis since the Second World War, comparatively few people make it to Britain in their search for safety.

In 2018, an estimated 612,000 people sought safety in Europe (down 11% from 2017).

Britain is not Europe's top recipient of asylum applications.

In 2018, many European countries received significantly higher numbers of asylum applications than the UK, with Germany and France receiving at least twice as many. In Germany alone, 154,000 asylum applications were made. Britain received approximately 6% of all asylum claims made in the EU in 2018.

The dreadful scenes still being witnessed in the Mediterranean and across Europe are a symptom of this wider, global crisis.

Throughout 2018, 107,192 people arrived in Europe via sea. Over a third were women and children.

Britain offers no asylum visa.

In point of fact there are very few, legal ways for refugees to safely escape their countries and claim asylum in another. When war breaks out, countries like Britain often close down refugees' legal escape routes. Refugees don't place their lives in smugglers' hands because they want to: they do it because they have no choice. The lack of safe and legal routes for refugees to reach safety and claim asylum has deadly results. In 2018, 2277 men, women and children lost their lives during desperate attempts to cross the Mediterranean Sea.

> World events often correlate directly with asylum applications; last year people were most likely to seek refuge here from the Middle East.

The top three countries of origin of people applying for asylum in Britain in 2018 were Iran, Iraq and Eritrea.

> People who are seeking asylum make up a tiny proportion of new arrivals in Britain.

In 2018, 20.5 million non-EEA nationals arrived in Britain, but only 0.14% of them were seeking refuge here (and not all those seeking asylum will be granted permission to stay).

> The British asylum system is extremely tough.

Only 33% of initial decisions in 2018 granted protection (asylum or humanitarian protection). However, many refugees had to rely on the courts rather than the government to afford them the protection they needed. The proportion of asylum appeals allowed through 2018 was 38%.

> Shockingly, by the quarter ending December 2018, 12,213 asylum applications had been waiting for longer than six months for an initial decision on the case.

This represented an increase of nearly 6% from the 11,538 applications of the previous quarter. The total backlog of cases pending a decision totalled 27,256, each one representing a person 'stuck in limbo'.

> The total number of unresolved cases over 36 months old (which in addition to cases awaiting initial decisions includes those cases awaiting an appeal outcome and those on hold, has been increasing continuously since 2014). As of the end of August 2018, these cases totalled 88,848.

> At the end of 2018, 50,143 people seeking asylum and their dependents were being supported by the government.

This figure has risen since 2012 but remains below the figure for the end of 2003, when there were 80,123 asylum seekers being supported. Support is typically minimal however, around £5 per day.

The UK government has the power to detain people who are here seeking refuge.

Over the last 12 months, 21,690 people were put in detention in an immigration removal centre, among them 12,637 people seeking asylum. 66% of all those detained in immigration removal centres were released back into the community (rendering their detention pointless).

In the 12 months up to December 2018, 63 children were put into immigration detention.

And this despite a government promise in 2010 to end the practice. 65% of the children who left detention were released (rendering their detention pointless).

Of the children who arrived in Britain alone and under their own steam, 49% were granted asylum in 2018.

This represented an increase from 35% at the end of the previous quarter. A further 15% of separated children were granted short-term leave to remain (which expires after 2.5 years, leaving them uncertain and anxious about the future). The top country of origin for new applications from unaccompanied children was Eritrea.

The number of people arriving from Syria who are resettled in Britain stands at 14,945 since the Vulnerable Persons Resettlement Scheme began.

In September 2015, Cameron promised to settle 20,000 Syrian refugees by 2020—just over 4000 per annum—but time is running out and at the time of writing no schemes for the future have been announced by his successor, May. Over 12 million people have been forcibly displaced from Syria since the commencement of the conflict, of whom more than 6.3 million are refugees.

The number of Syrians who have sought asylum in Britain since the conflict began stands at just 10,382.

> This represents just 0.16% of Syria's refugees. 'Like most of the world's refugees, very few Syrians come to Britain in their search for safety'.
>
> In 2018, just 693 non-Syrian refugees were resettled in Britain via the Gateway Protection Programme run in conjunction with the UN's Refugee Agency (UNHCR).
>
> A mere 1% of the world's refugees will ever be resettled, which means that many refugees face a protracted, anxious wait to hear if they will be able to rebuild their lives in safety.
>
> War and persecution often divides refugees from their families, but there are few straightforward, legal ways for refugees to safely join loved ones in Britain.
>
> One way in which refugees could be allowed to travel to the UK safely is through the Mandate scheme. This enables refugees in other countries to join their family members in Britain. But this route is rarely used by the government, with only 18 refugees arriving via the scheme during 2018.
>
> Another safe and legal route for refugees to safely join their loved ones in the UK is via refugee family reunion visas.
>
> In 2018, 5900 of these visas were issued to partners and children of those granted asylum or humanitarian protection in the UK. This is an increase of 13% from 2017.
>
> Adapted from Refugee Council (2019).

This explicit and politically expedient 'othering' of strangers, who are portrayed as irrational at best, cunning at worst, betrays the mindset and class habitus of the British power elite. It reflects the class and command relations emanating in the class/command dynamic adumbrated earlier. Javid redefined those attempting the perilous crossing of the English Channel as 'illegal immigrants', in the process corrupting any prior international commitment to refugees' rights. But this is not just down to relations of class and command. Those of gender and ethnicity or race are key causal mechanisms. With regard to race, which is of course especially salient for any consideration of refugees, Amin (2012: 88) writes of an interplay between 'phenotypical racism' and 'racial biopolitics':

the claim ... is that it is the interplay between phenotypical racism ... – exemplified by a historical vernacular of reading social worth from bodily differences – and racial biopolitics, that critically affects the real experience of race, arbitrating between stranger tolerance and aversion ... The collapse of multiculturalism and the rapid spread of xenophobic sentiment today are explained as the result of reinforcing feedbacks between everyday habits of judgement, guided by ingrained legacies of white superiority and an unashamedly punitive state politics of surveillance and discipline of the stranger that has emerged since 9/11.

Amin's claim resonates with sociological explanations of Brexit. The class politics of financial capitalism reflect a resurgent, post-multiculturalist— and in relation to the class/command dynamic, functional—narrative of xenophobia and white supremacy, leading to an altogether harsher, fundamentalist and unforgiving environment for migrants and refugees alike. The cultural ethos pointing positively towards diversity and recognition has faded.

Consider the lot and experiences of those 'detained' in the Immigration Removal Centre at Yarl's Wood (*Independent*, 2019). Approximately 120 women, out of the 410 detained in Yarl's Wood, went on strike over 'inhumane' conditions. One Algerian woman said: 'every day I wake up and I have to think of a reason to go on. I've given up thinking about the outside—I've given up thinking about it. I feel like I'm in someone's dungeon and no one is letting me out. I might as well be blindfolded in a van going at 100 miles an hour in a direction I don't know. The indefinite detention causes people so much stress. People are breaking down psychologically. We have no fight left. They break you down. It's inhumane' (*Independent*, 2019). Another detainee from Kenya said she had developed stomach problems and had no alternative but to stop eating (she had lost 10 kg).

The women on hunger strike produced a document accusing the Home Office of violating *habeas corpus*, as most detainees are not detained by a judge. They also objected that the government has refused to acknowledge that rape is a form of torture: rape victims are detained despite a policy statement in 2016 that victims of torture must not be detained for reasons relating to immigration. The women noted too that the UK is the only country in the EU with no time limit on detention, and appended a charge of widespread incompetence. The charity Women for Refugee Women has found that 85% of the women who had sought asylum and been detained since the policy statement of 2016 were survivors of rape or other gender-based violence, including forced marriage, female genital mutilation and coerced prostitution. HM Inspectorate of Prisons has also raised concerns about the continued detention of these women.

This is a clear illustration of the causal relevance of enduring social structures or relations to the day-to-day dilemmas and suffering of would-be refugees making it to Britain. Class and the class/command dynamic underpin financial capitalism's global reach, geopolitics, not least in the Middle East and Africa, and privileging of profit over justice and human solidarity. As is apparent through the history of gender and racial and ethnic relations, it is women rather than men, and non-white women especially, who bear the brunt of the suffering, extending from feminised and racialised poverty to open brutality. *The racialisation of fear* is key. Amin (2012: 102–103) once more:

> 'The administration of disaster' as a 'form of governance' and a way of ruling, involving the suspension of 'citizenship, the system of law and the constitution itself', is being taken for granted as states of emergency cease to be seen as states of exception …Whatever the causes of the contemporary scaling up of punitive biopolitics (from anxieties of globalisation to the politics of life or catastrophe management), the new tactics of order, playing on popular fear and aversion towards people considered different or anomalous, are allowing all manner of vengeance to be thrown at the racialised stranger ….

'Weaponising Stigma'

These short excursions on the long term ill and disabled and migrants and refugees invite an extension of the Goffmanesque explication of stigma and of my observations on deviance presented earlier in this volume. Account must be taken of macro- and meso- as well as micro-level structures. Stigma and deviance, involving infringements against norms of shame (an ontological deficit) and blame (a moral deficit) respectively, need to be revisited. Reference to the weaponising of stigma directs attention to a wilful political strategy of 'heaping blame on shame', or rendering people personally responsible for their 'problems', whatever form these might take (impoverishment, homelessness, disability and so on). Critically, stigma weaponised in such a fashion opens the way for

Table 5.4 The dialectic between shame and blame (Scambler, 2018b)

Stigma + deviance + *Abjects*	Stigma + deviance − *Rejects*
Stigma − deviance − *Normals*	Stigma − deviance + *Losers*

governments to abandon any collective responsibility for helping them, cutting benefits and so on.

Consider the typology in Table 5.4, articulated as follows. Stigma + deviance − = *rejects*; stigma + deviance + = *abjects*; stigma − deviance + = *losers*; and stigma − deviance − = *normals*. These rather grim labels might be ranked according to their functionality for neoliberal class-driven governance. Thus, the effective attribution of the label 'abjects' affords the most latitude for exploitation and oppression; next comes 'losers'; then 'rejects' (among whom abjects might of course be recruited).

It takes the kind of power that only capital can buy—though further warped by pre-existing gender and race/ethnic relations—to re-write norms of shame and blame towards abjection, and there is always resistance to be subdued and overcome. The mainstream media that are most persuasive in the public sphere (in Habermasian terms, the most 'influential') play a critical role. When these are overwhelmingly in the hands of (non-dom, non tax-paying, 'nomadic') neoliberals with a vested interest in easing the way to further capital accumulation, resistance is made all the more difficult. To these media might be added the right-wing think tanks that fuel them (see Slater, 2018). The principal characteristics of the think tanks currying favour and carrying influence in the public sector of the lifeworld are summarised in Table 5.5.

Table 5.5 Dark money, dirty politics and think tanks

Dark money, a familiar term in US politics, refers to those monies clandestinely invested to warp democratic processes like elections. Dark money disseminates 'ideology' (a world view that reflects particular vested interests) at the expense of 'knowledge' (an evidence-based world view that reflects applications of the scientific project) (that all scientific knowledge is fallible is true but quite another matter). Think tanks are crucial devices for disseminating ideology.

One route to influence in the public sphere of the lifeworld, a form of 'lifeworld colonisation' in Habermas' terminology, is via the funding of think tanks. Some of the most influential think tanks are listed below, together with (a) their political orientation, and (b) their degree of transparency re-their funders. I have taken as a measure of transparency a rating from A (totally open) to E (totally closed) deployed by the 'UK Campaign for Think Tank Transparency'. (A) indicates that the think tank is open about its income, displays funding details on its website, names funders, and declares the amounts given. (E) indicates that the think tank fails *all* these tests.

Adam Smith Institute (ASI)
  Main focus of the ASI is the introduction of free-market policies. (E)
Centre for Policy Studies (CPS)
  Founded by Thatcher in 1974, the CPS aims to promote free-market policies and limit the role of the state. (E)
Centre for Social Justice (CSJ)
  Established by Duncan Smith in 2004 to seek solutions to social breakdown and poverty, with a focus on the voluntary sector combatting poverty. (D)
Demos
  Founded in 1993, Demos is a cross-party think tank interested in welfare and public services, education, citizenship and social media. (B)
Fabian Society
  Founded in 1884 and affiliated to the Labour Party, the Fabian Society is a major left-of-centre think tank. (A)
Institute for Economic Affairs (IEA)
  One of the oldest in the UK, the IEA is a high-profile right-wing think tank that promotes free-market solutions to a wide range of social and economic issues. (E)

High Pay Centre (HPC)
Set up to monitor top levels of pay. (A)
Institute for Fiscal Studies (IFS)
Established to provide independent research on economic and fiscal policy. (A)
Institute for Public Policy Research (IPPR)
Was formed following Labour's 1987 election defeat, aiming to invigorate leftwing thinking. (B)
The Legatum Institute
Set up as an international, right-of-centre liberal think tank focused on revitalising capitalism and democracy. (C)
New Economics Foundation (NEF)
An independent, left-of-centre 'think and do' think tank that aims to promote alternative economic models, focusing also on social justice and environmental issues. (A)
Policy Exchange
A right-wing small-government think tank that conducts research into poverty and social mobility, public services and economic issues. (E)
Reform
An independent right-of-centre think tank that seeks to set out a way to lower public spending and increase prosperity. (C)
Resolution Foundation
Founded in 2005 to produce high-quality research and raise the profile of the challenges facing those on low to middle incomes and to develop policy solutions. (B)
Social Market Foundation (SMF)
The SMF is an independent, liberal think tank that aims to combine market economics with social justice. (B)
Tax Justice Network
Launched in 2003 as an independent, left-of-centre and 'activist' think tank to push for 'justice' and systematic change in relation to tax, tax havens and financial globalisation. (A)
TaxPayers' Alliance (TPA)
A right-wing think tank established in 2004 to campaign for lower taxation and for reducing public expenditure. (E)

This list comprises some of the main, 'loudest' and most influential think tanks. Two immediate points are in order. First, it will be apparent that those described as right-of-centre or right wing are the least transparent re-funding [almost all of them rating an (E)], while those towards the opposite end of the political spectrum are characterised by a much greater degree of transparency (almost all of them rating an (A). And second, it must be remarked that the mainstream media, having long since abandoned the expertise found in academia, rely increasingly on representatives from think tanks. This being so, the—often ideological—allegiances of these spokespersons are a matter of huge import. *Who is paying them to say what, and in whose interests?* Currently, right-wing think tanks are conspicuously over-represented in the mainstream media.

Slater (2014) has shown how one right-wing think tank, the Centre for Social Justice (CSJ), founded by Iain Duncan Smith (architect of Universal Credit), has invoked a littany of social pathologies (family breakdown, worklessness, antisocial behaviour, personal irresponsibility, out-of-wedlock childbirth, dependency) *to manufacture ignorance* and rationalise welfare 'reform' (i.e. benefit cuts).

Slater (2018) has also exposed the role of another right-wing think tank, Policy Exchange, in what he calls 'agnotology, or the intentional production of ignorance'. He shows how Policy Exchange has campaigned to attribute what he calls 'territorial stigma' to living spaces castigated as 'sink estates', thereby allowing people living in such environments to be neglected, 'sanctioned', punished or worse. And this is all part and parcel of a more generalised assault on public housing.

Dark money and clandestinely-funded right-wing think tanks are means or *devices* that allow individual members of the hard core of our (transnational, nomadic) capitalist executive to make their purchase of policies conducive to the further accumulation of their capital from the state's power elite acceptable to the public. What all this does is further expose the deep underlying social structures and relations of class and class conflict. *Denial of class conflict is itself a manifestation of that conflict.*

The following observations pave the way for the final chapter in this volume, which amends traditional sociological frames encompassing shaming and blaming:

- The dialectic between stigma and deviance varies from context to context, or, *pace* Elias, from figuration to figuration (e.g. from class-derived neoliberal ideology via gendered and racialised local pay scales to the everyday dynamics of neighbourhood gangs).
- Only rarely does this dialectic operate to the detriment of the wealthy and powerful.
- The wealthy and powerful should not be studied and appraised as individuals, but rather in terms of the 'deep' social structures and relations they surf to their advantage.
- Structures and relations should be treated as topic- as well as context- or figuration-specific.
- Generative mechanisms pertinent to the weaponising of stigma are emergent in cultural and agential as well as structural relations.
- These mechanisms generally operate without interruption, but (a) their expected effects on events can be cancelled out by countervailing mechanisms (as well as free will and happenstance); (b) they cannot be directly observed; and (c) they cannot be simply read straight off from patterns of events; so (d) their existence has to be 'inferred' from the findings of quantitative and qualitative research.
- The sociological project runs from micro- through meso- to macro-processes.
- A non-reductionist sociology can discern causally compelling mechanisms linking the likes of transnational corporations, capital flows and Brexit with 'hunger pains', foodbank usage, loneliness, depression and bodily impairment and collapse.

Post-Goffman's dramaturgy there is a challenge to innovate theoretically and conceptually to accommodate a more comprehensive agenda of the kind outlined here. In the next chapter, I accent what I earlier called *metareflection*, that is, pausing to think through what we already know, both theoretically and substantively, and to optimise use of existing resources. More imaginative bridge-building between theoretical and empirical discourses is especially important.

References

Amin, A. (2012). *Land of strangers*. Cambridge: Polity Press.
Bukodi, E., & Goldthorpe, J. (2019). *Social mobility and education in Britain*. Cambridge: Cambridge University Press.
Carroll, W. (2008). The corporate elite and the transformation of financial capital. In M. Savage & K. Williams (Eds.), *Remembering elites* (pp. 49–62). Oxford: Blackwell.
Castells, M. (2019). *Rupture: The crisis of liberal democracy*. Cambridge: Polity Press.
Clark, T., & Heath, A. (2014). *Hard times: The divisive toll of the economic slump*. New Haven, CT: Yale University Press.
Clement, W., & Myles, J. (1997). *Relations of ruling: Class and gender in postindustrial societies*. Toronto: McGill Queen's University Press.
Davis, A. (2018). *Reckless opportunists: Elites at the end of the establishment*. Manchester: Manchester University Press.
Habermas, J. (1975). *Legitimation crisis*. London: Heinemann.
Habermas, J. (1989). *The new conservatism*. Cambridge: Cambridge University Press.
Independent. (2019). More than 100 women in Yarl's Wood detention centre go on hunger strike over 'inhumane' conditions. https://www.independent.co.uk/home-news/yarls-wood-women...ration-detention-centre-hunger-strike-home-office-a8223886.html. Accessed 14 March 2019.
Landes, D. (1998). *Wealth and poverty of nations*. London: Little, Brown & Co.
Mills, C. W. (1956). *The power elite*. New York: Oxford University Press.
Observer Editorial. (2019). The Observer view on Britain failing dismally in its moral duty to help refugees. https://www.theguardian.com/commentisfree/2019/jan/06/observer-view-on-britain-failing-in-moral-duty-to-help-refugees. Accessed 14 March 2019.
Piketty, T. (2014). *Capital in the twenty-first century*. Cambridge, MA: Harvard University Press.
Refugee Council. (2019). *Top 20 facts about refugees and people seeking asylum*. https://www.refugeecouncil.org.uk/topfacts. Accessed 12 March 2019.
Scambler, G. (2012). Archer, morphogenesis and the role of agency in the sociology of health inequalities. In G. Scambler (Ed.), *Contemporary theorists for medical sociology* (pp. 131–149). London: Routledge.
Scambler, G. (2018a). *Sociology, health and the fractured society: A critical realist account*. London: Routledge.
Scambler, G. (2018b). Heaping blame on shame: 'Weaponising stigma' for neoliberal times. *Sociological Review, 66*, 766–782.

Scambler, G., & Scambler, S. (2015). Theorising health inequalities: The untapped potential of dialectical critical realism. *Social Theory and Health, 13,* 340–354.

Slater, T. (2014). The myth of 'Broken Britain': Welfare reform and the production of ignorance. *Antipode, 46,* 948–969.

Slater, T. (2018). The invention of the 'sink estate': Consequential categorisation and the UK housing crisis. *Sociological Review, 66,* 877–897.

Thomas, C. (2007). *Sociologies of illness and disability: Contested ideas in disability studies and medical sociology.* Basingstoke: Palgrave Macmillan.

CHAPTER 6

Towards a Sociology of Shaming and Blaming

Abstract This chapter considers stigma and deviance as forms of vulnerability and goes on to comment on and extend existing sociological descriptions and explanations of stigma. The salience of money and power is emphasised and the chapter discusses how these system steering media combine in financial capitalism to convert shame into blame in line with political agendas. Attention is also paid to ways of resisting this weaponising of stigma. As is the case throughout the book, much use is made of the four groups selected as foci, namely migrants and refugees, the long-term sick and disabled, the homeless and sex workers.

Keywords Vulnerability · System steering media · Money · Power · Weaponising stigma

So used are we to the blandishments and exhortations of the multiple forms of individualism that have pervaded contemporary culture and our lifeworlds that we only too easily overlook their ideological roots and their systemic functionality for the capital executive and their allies and co-optees. Individual experiences are of both intrinsic and extrinsic values to sociologists, the former because sociology is nothing if not compassionate, engaged and committed to the betterment of people's lives, the latter because sociologists focus on the detection and enunciation of those social structures and relations that help causally to fashion the individuals that we spend our lives 'becoming' (to borrow a Sartrean term).

Among the subpopulations of migrants and refugees, the long-term ill and disabled, the homeless and sex workers discussed in previous chapters there exists considerable heterogeneity; moreover, not all are shamed and blamed in the same ways or to the same degree. It is a very different matter to work the streets conspicuously as a sex worker than to work more discretely as an escort from a rented apartment; nor do the experiences of either reduce to simple formulae. But it is the task of sociologists to infer via substantive research or metareflection which social mechanisms are causally telling for their phenomena of concern, in this case for processes of shaming and blaming. Data are forthcoming from a wide range of sources, from case studies to what critical realists term the 'demi-regs' of quantification.

It must be remembered too that a multiplicity of social mechanisms operate in an open society; can exercise countervailing powers; co-exist with biological and psychological mechanisms; and are subject to the 'interference' of contingency and agentic causality. A smidgeon of humility on the part of the sociologist is therefore called for. A further illustration of the complexity that sociologists face might be apt.

Take the diagnosis of epilepsy, which has since ancient times typically signalled possession of a stigmatised identity. In medical textbooks and practice, epilepsy denotes a tendency to recurrent seizures, and seizures can take a variety of different forms, some—like 'grand mal'—conspicuous, and others—like 'petit mal'—less so. Its aetiology still frequently uncertain, epilepsy is a symptom not a disease. Hopkins (1987: 124–125) makes the following observation on causality:

> Consider a man with a moderate genetic disposition to seizures. Add the effects of a moderate cranial injury some two years before. Add also the effects of 'stress' at the office during the preceding month. Add also the effects of amitriptyline prescribed to help with the depression associated with this stress. If this man then has a seizure after consuming a moderate amount of alcohol the night before, what caused it – the genetic propensity, the cranial injury, the stress, the alcohol and associated metabolic changes, the disturbance of sleep associated with the depression, or the amitriptyline? Depending upon the perspective of the world of both patient and neurologist, agreement may be reached to blame just one or all of these factors, quite illogically.

Now consider 'living with epilepsy' and what is commonly called 'epilepsy-related quality of life' (ERQOL), suspending for the moment concerns about the limitations and distortions of conceptualisations of long-term illness based on the personal tragedy paradigm. In my own contributions, I have acknowledged that biological mechanisms, extending from genetics to the neuropharmacology of antiepileptic medication, typically *matter* with regard to ERQOL, deepening understanding often mitigating epilepsy's assault on people's day-to-day lives via more effective treatment. Yet even severe biological insults 'may not' be decisive for ERQOL. Psychological mechanisms typically *condition* people's handling of epilepsy's assault and, therefore, its impact on ERQOL, independently of biological severity or intractability. There is considerable scope for counselling, for targeting the interface between enduring psychological states and coping styles. Yet psychological mechanisms also 'may not' be decisive for ERQOL. It is social mechanisms that typically provide people with *contexts*, some of which can be critical for ERQOL. Most dramatically, as long as epilepsy remains undiagnosed by a state-sanctioned and licensed medical practitioner, then the potentially stigmatising identity of 'epileptic' can be avoided (alternatively, a physician's misdiagnosis of epilepsy can inflict this same identity in the absence of signs and/or symptoms). Less dramatically, spontaneous reactions to a witnessed seizures on the part of family, friends or strangers can prove pivotal in the long as well as short term. But social mechanisms too 'may not' be compelling for ERQOL (see Scambler, Afentouli, & Selai, 2010).

Into this mix must be inserted social mechanisms around stigma. In my 'hidden distress model' of epilepsy, I emphasised the role of felt stigma, referring to a sense of shame and a fear of encountering stigmatisation on the grounds of unacceptable difference (enacted stigma). Felt stigma frequently disposes to a wary secrecy and can compromise aspiration. The desire for secrecy also leads to routine concealment of the diagnosis, to decisions to pass as normal, and these in turn reduce opportunities for enacted stigma. I drew on Bourdieu to postulate an 'epilepsy habitus', namely an enduring, context-induced mindset informed primarily by felt stigma, which predisposes people to submit to, or remain passive in the face of, disadvantaging difference. Anticipating enacted stigma, people with epilepsy often (learn to) do to themselves what they anticipate others will inevitably do to them if given the opportunity. An epilepsy habitus can develop independently of either biological or psychological mechanisms, though it too might lose salience for ERQOL in the presence of, for example, uncompromising biological (e.g. severe brain injury) or psychological (e.g. a strong internal locus of control) mechanisms (Scambler, 2018a).

So sociological explorations of shaming and blaming are necessarily bounded and circumscribed. Having captured something of the complexity implicit in such projects, this final chapter is divided into three main sections. The first insists that shaming and blaming—stigma and deviance—comprise two of a number of distinguishable forms of exclusion, othering or vulnerability. It is argued that such forms tend to cluster and can rarely be accounted for in isolation. The second section is devoted to the overriding significance of power in shaming and blaming. It is in this section that the arguments of the book are summarised in terms of discrete theses. Finally, attention is given to: (a) agential causal efficacy and (b) modes of resistance to shaming and blaming in today's fractured society, the product of an era of financial capitalism whose days many sociologists deem to be numbered.

Forms of Vulnerability

I have contended elsewhere that vulnerability relevant to health and wellbeing can assume different guises and disguises (Scambler, 2018c). Eight of these forms or dimensions of vulnerability—I am omitting stigma and deviance, which have already been defined—are also pertinent here and are as follows:

- *Anomie*: It was Durkheim (1897) who recognised the sense of 'being lost' in the 'normless' social world that marked the structural, cultural and agential transition from the mechanical solidarity of traditional societies to the organic solidarity of modern industrial capitalism. Anomie, if in amended form, has unquestionably survived into financial capitalism.
- *Alienation*: For Marx, people in capitalism become thing-like, mere cogs in the unforgiving machinery of production. Workers become alienated from their product, from the process of production, from their very nature as humans, and from other workers as they are themselves transmuted into commodities. Like anomie, alienation has retained its relevance.
- *Powerlessness*: anomie and alienation can each be cause or effect of powerlessness. For Bourdieu (1980), powerlessness amounts to a lack of those forms of capital—economic, cultural and social—that are the prerequisites of effective influence across numerous fields or contexts. Lack of capital induces vulnerability.

- *Marginalisation*: as well as each of the subpopulations discussed in this book, other putative 'misfits' like the members of Roma communities can fall into this category. Pushed to the edge of society, it comprises people routinely othered and represented by stereotypes replete with errors of commission and omission. Trump's treatment of would-be refugees, extending to separating children from their parents, is another case in point.
- *Exclusion*: Exclusion is an umbrella term and can take many forms, but there emerged in the 1990s an expedient 'third way' political rhetoric of 'social exclusion' that served to disguise, and in the process neuter, inconvenient talk of long-term structural inequalities. It was associated with policy initiatives focused on 'social inclusion' that exhorted personal responsibility.
- *Cultural imperialism*: This echoes historical and imperialist notions of racial or ethnic superiority and superordinance in relation to those seen as inferior or subordinate. Much racism recalls past institutions of extreme purposeful violence, slavery and exploitation. Racism is often a product of cultural imperialism and frequently translates into 'internal colonialism'. It is readily apparent in the social orbits and politics of Trump in the USA and Farage, May and Johnson in the UK.
- *Loneliness*: Like suicide, loneliness strikes as an intensely individual—or psychological—phenomenon, but it too as strong social determinants. Older people in Japan, for example, remain absorbed in extended families, while in other countries they are abandoned in the wake of enhanced social and geographical mobility, welfare fragmentation and hyper-individualism.
- *Symbolic violence*: Bourdieu's (1980) use of this term recognises that coercive force is often not required for hegemonic ideologies to prevail. Politico-social groundwork and 'soft power' can typically deliver, rendering explicit threats redundant. Conspiracies are relatively scarce due to the importance and effectiveness of a combination of what Bourdieu (1980) called a 'class habitus' and what C. W. Mills (1956) referred to as 'tacit understanding'.

Even with the additions of stigmatisation and deviance, there is no pretence that this list is exhaustive. The point of its inclusion is merely to emphasise that the sources of vulnerability are multiple. They also overlap: none is stand-alone. Moreover, they can be causally interrelated in complex ways. Alienation can lead to loneliness even as it is (mis)represented as a 'natural' age-related mode of social exclusion or as an outcome of chance events. Cultural imperialism can transmute into the deliberate and political creation of a 'hostile environment', as in the UK's Windrush Scandal, in the process complementing vulnerability via a newfound powerlessness. A Roma community, already marginalised, can find itself newly answerable to a weaponising of stigma. It is important to acknowledge that: (a) these types of vulnerability are not mutually exclusive; (b) for those made vulnerable in *any* of these ways, or indeed in other ways, the precise mode and/or source of vulnerability is generally unimportant; and (c) it is for sociologists that such categorisations carry weight and analytic import.

How is this tentative typology of forms of vulnerability relevant to the subpopulations or groups featured here? Well, consider sex workers. I have drawn on my own research to appraise how the 'whore stigma' can seep into the lifeworlds of migrant escort workers cast as opportunists. Given the prevailing sex work hierarchy, it might reasonably be concluded that visible, 'discredited' street workers might be most subject to stigmatisation, via enacted stigma and deviance; yet invisible, 'discreditable' escort workers too cannot escape, via felt stigma and deviance. Only one of those I interviewed in my study had told her parents how she earned a living. Families, sex worker clients too, can be affected by what Goffman calls 'courtesy stigma', or the contagious spread of the whore stigma.

The Pivotal Roles of Money and Power, and Foucault's Addendum

Money and power, for Habermas, are the steering media of the economy and the state, respectively. It is through these media that the system has colonised and in financial capitalism continues to colonise the lifeworld. Through the implicit formulae of the class/command dynamic, that is, that money buys the power to make policy, it has been argued above that macro-structures constrain 'the many' even as they enable 'the few' (to borrow some felicitous phrasing). More than this, such structures provide parameters within which most people for most of their lifespans 'take decisions' about their selves and their projects. In this way is free will hemmed in.

The link between power and shaming and blaming has been forcefully emphasised in the recent literature, usually under the generalised rubric of the sociology of stigma. Link and Phelan (2001: 363) draw on both sociological and disability studies to define stigma as 'the co-occurrence of its components – labelling, stereotyping, separation, status loss, and discrimination'. They add that for stigmatisation to occur *power must be exercised*. They deploy the term discrimination sociologically and distinctively: it does not refer to one individual's treatment of another but to structural or institutional discrimination (e.g. a 'disabling environment'), and to discrimination one or more steps removed from labelling and stereotyping, as when a loss of status occasioned by stigmatisation leads to a spiralling of disadvantage. They insist that 'stigma is entirely dependent on social, economic, and political power – *it takes power to stigmatise*' (emphasis added) (Link & Phelan, 2001: 375; and see Scambler 2009).

Link and Phelan's explication of stigma poses a number of questions:

- Do those who might stigmatise have sufficient power to ensure the human difference they recognise and label resonates in the public culture?
- Do those who might confer stigma have the power to ensure that the culture 'deeply accepts' the stereotypes they connect to labelled differences?
- Do those who might stigmatise possess power enough to underwrite and maintain a separation of 'us' from 'them'?
- Do those who might confer stigma have the power to control access to core institutions like schooling, job markets, housing and healthcare in order to 'put really consequential teeth into the distinctions they draw'?

Affirmative answers to this quartet of queries, Link and Phelan contend, would lead us to expect stigma, while negative responses would generally preclude it.

Parker and Aggleton (2003) call in similar vein for a post-individualist analysis of stigma, focusing on the process on HIV/AIDS. In this case, they argue, stigma functions 'at the point of intersection between *culture, power and difference*'. Relations of stigma are central to the constitution of the social order; and the social order 'promotes the interests of dominant groups as well as distinctions and hierarchies of ranking between them, while legitimating that ranking by convincing the dominated to accept existing hierarchies through processes of hegemony'.

Jacquet's criteria of 'effective stigmatisation', outlined in Table 6.1, complement Link and Phelan's and Parker and Aggleton's, but betray a psychological rather than a sociological thrust. The emphases they add are that the public must care about what is at stake; that the gap between the desirable and undesirable must be significant; that a body of formal sanctioning should not already be in place; that the individual(s) must be sensitive to and 'trust' the source of the shaming; and that the shaming must be targetted, imposed and policed efficiently for maximum effect. Jacquet's explication is reflective of (social) psychological mechanisms at play in processes of shaming as well as the kind of social mechanisms indicated by Link and Phelan.

Table 6.1 Jacquet's criteria for effective stigmatisation (Jacquet, 2015)

1. The audience responsible for the shaming should be concerned with the transgression;
2. There should be a big gap between the desired and actual behaviour;
3. Formal punishment should be missing;
4. The transgressor should be sensitive to the source of the shaming;
5. The audience should trust the source of the shaming;
6. Shaming should be directed where possible benefits are greatest;
7. Scrupulous implementation.

Accenting the core salience of power relations for shaming and blaming significantly revises the analysis. To this point, power has been introduced principally as the medium by means of which the state contributes to what Habermas calls system rationalisation, or the systemic colonisation of the lifeworld. And it has been emphasised that—increasingly through the post-1970s financialised capitalism—the power possessed by the state has become more answerable to the steering medium of money, representing the economy in general and the capital executive and its capital monopolists in particular. Implicitly, it is *power as domination* that has provided the focus, reflecting the approach of critical theorists in the tradition of the Frankfurt School like Habermas. While it is regrettable that the exercise of power as dominance is largely absent in the writings of Foucault, there is no doubt that the latter's concept of 'disciplinary power' and his deployment of innovative notions like 'technologies of the self', 'governmentality' and 'surveillance', can significantly deepen sociologies of power. For me, it is as if: (a) power as dominance is represented by a river and (b) disciplinary power is to be found amongst the river's tributaries.

Possibly the optimum way of illustrating the purchase of this complex assembly of perspectives on both vulnerability and power, and their critical input into a sociology of shaming and blaming, is through a fictitious case study that resonates with substantive research. I draw here on an adaptation of a case study presented elsewhere (Scambler, 2018c).

> Marcia's grandfather came over to London in the early 1960s in response to an advert for bus drivers placed in a local newspaper in Jamaica. He was joined later by his wife and their two children, one of whom was to become Marcia's mother. The family were met with a degree of racial prejudice and hostility but this was compensated for by the supportive closeness of the black community and 'subculture' in South London. By the mid-1970s, in a more competitive job market, Marcia's father found himself out of work and under material and other pressures her parents split up. Marcia was aged two when this occurred (and is now in her early 40s). She left school at 16 and worked in a local supermarket prior to meeting her partner and moving to rental accommodation outside of 'her' neighbourhood. She has had two children with her partner. She works as a hospital cleaner but her hours have been cut, she has no sick or holiday pay and no work-related pension to look forward to; and her partner has only found occasional temporary work. Her daughter, with whom she was very close, moved away to attend a northern university and has since found work and set up home there. Her son has been less fortunate, has struggled during and between zero-hours contracts and still lives with Marcia and her partner. He is currently unemployed and his GP has diagnosed a depressive disorder. Life has become a struggle for this trio, the more so since the introduction and ramping up of policies of 'austerity' since 2010. The benefits they were once entitled were cut back, and they are losing out again with the rolling out universal credit. They have had no benefit payments now for over a month, they are behind with the rent, their landlord, an MP, is threatening

them with eviction. Despite considerable reluctance they have begun to rely on provisions from the local foodbank. Marcia's partner and son have been told they must demonstrate a will to work or continue to suffer the consequences, this despite the fact that her partner daily searches for any form of paid work. The outlook is bleak. Marcia voted for Brexit in the referendum - 'We need change. We can't go on like this!' - but now fears the possible consequences. The omens seem bleak and Marcia herself finds it harder and harder to hold things together, let alone retain any sense of optimism for the future. She is glad her daughter 'escaped'. It seems like the final straw that a week ago she received an official letter from the Home Office challenging her right to remain in Britain in the absence of any written proof of her entitlement to do so.

Marcia's vulnerability is readily apparent, most obviously via alienation, anomie, stigmatisation and the weaponising of stigma by means of its transmutation into abjection by the addition of deviance. It is clear too that the class/command dynamic is causally implicated in this vulnerability: it is key to the immiseration strategically visited on Marcia and her family. But the class/command dynamic is far from the whole story. Racial/ethnic and gender relations are core to the unfolding of Marcia's biography as are other dimensions of vulnerability. She must surely experience, feel and embody powerlessness, marginalisation and, not least on her daughter's departure, loneliness. What her story notably invites too is a focus on cultural imperialism and symbolic violence. Britain remains as demonstrably racist as it is 'multicultural': rhetorical resort to apparently liberal commendations of 'multiculturalism' can serve to conceal or camouflage this, not always innocently. Marcia, enlightened by her family's oral history, is reflexive as well as fatalistic about this. Her lived experience in the South London's lifeworld is of cultural imperialism and internal colonialism, somewhat less conspicuous since her grandparents' arrival in the 1960s but incontrovertibly more vital post-Brexit and now epitomised—cruelly caricatured in fact—in the correspondence from the Home Office. The Windrush scandal, personally sponsored by British Prime Minister and former Home Secretary, Theresa May, and at the cutting edge of an explicitly racist government policy to create a 'hostile environment' for those migrants unable to buy their way to citizenship, feels to Marcia like a final nail in her family's coffin. It is the actualisation of Bourdieu's (1980) symbolic violence.

Marcia's case is far from exceptional: it is statistically commonplace. She is not merely rendered vulnerable by her colour and heritage, her gender is also causally critical. Hospital cleaning is as low-paid as it is socially important and employees are disproportionately women, most notably women from ethnic minorities. These segments of the working population have long provided cheap labour, a trend not only perpetuated but exploited yet further by private contractors for whom oppressive governments since 1979 have acted as agents. In the era of financial capitalism, working conditions, comprising security as well as pay and conditions, have been systematically eroded; and this has maximal effect on occupations dominated by female labour. Financial capitalism runs along deep grooves carved out by gender as well as race and ethnic relations and long pre-existing capitalism's birth in the long sixteenth century. Women, and the more so women from ethnic minority communities, are still 'cabin'd, cribbed, confined and bound in' by ubiquitous swathes of institutional varieties of symbolic violence no less damaging than in times of coercive 'sovereign' power.

The account offered in Scambler (2018c) can be revisited and extended in the light of the present sharper focus on shaming and blaming. In my view, a sociology of shaming and blaming should comprise a number of interrelated elements, recognising that:

- Shaming and blaming have their taproots in the statics and dynamics of social systems. Theoretically and conceptually, Habermas' system/lifeworld distinction provides a convenient peg on which to hang a credible analysis of the salience of system rationalisation and colonisation for shaming and blaming.
- Class relations in Habermas' economic subsystem, issuing in exploitation, together with the command relations in the subsystem of the state, issuing in oppression, are the principal structures or mechanisms in financial capitalism that fuel shaming and blaming.
- Other relations, like those of gender, issuing in sexism, and race or ethnicity, issuing in racism, also exercise a major causal influence, both *in line with* those of class and command and independently of them. Other structures or mechanisms, like age (leading to ageism), also fall into this category.
- Relations like those of class, command, gender, race/ethnicity and age *elide into*—and the distinction here is neither sharp nor definitive—others no less significant for shaming and blaming but perhaps most aptly characterised as the progeny of post-1960s 'human rights discourse' and 'identity politics'. This category subsumes people with dis-abilities (leading to dis-ablism) and those living with 'post-binary' sexualities (leading, e.g., to homophobia).

- Social structures or relations, on a spectrum from class and command to those around rights and identities, contribute to and reflect cultural norms; that is, the relationship between them is properly dialectical. However, echoing Marx, it is structure rather than culture that *tends* to prevail.
- Notwithstanding the (structural) thrust of these comments so far, in the course of financial capitalism, cultural norms have undoubtedly 'intruded', imposed themselves upon, and in the process camouflaged those of structure. Bourdieu's notion of class habitus retains its explanatory power; *but* it's become less apparent or conspicuous.
- The subsystem of the state, coalescing around a power elite variably responsive or amenable to 'shaping' via other structures, most notably class, is the ultimate site of responsibility for the enactment of legislation pertinent to shaming and blaming. Such legislation can either legitimate or render enacted stigma and/or deviance illegal.
- Laws have unintended as well as intended consequences, as, for example, with laws on sex work in Britain which, while not defining sex work as illegal, in practice circumscribe and constrain it to the point at which many indoor and most outdoor workers are permanently vulnerable.
- A key weapon in the state's execution of its power in financial capitalism has taken the form of appending blame to shame or 'weaponising stigma'. A perfect storm, allowing for maximum pressure for the othering or estrangement of segments of the population, is accomplished through 'abjection' (see also Tyler, 2013). As was made clear in Table 5.4 on the dialectic between shame and blame, the abject is deemed both ontologically and morally beyond the pale and therefore beyond (worthwhile or effective state) help. For the state, moral deficits trump ontological deficits, allowing for a ranking from most to least susceptible to oppression: (1) abjects (stigma + deviance +), (2) losers (stigma − deviance +), (3) rejects (stigma + deviance −) and, with by far the best array of defences, (4) normals (stigma − deviance −).
- In the context of this treatise stigma has been weaponised most brutally and effectively in relation to refugees, the disabled and the homeless, who have been all but abandoned 'American-style' (see Wacquant's (2008) study of overwhelmingly black working-class rejects inhabiting a ghetto on the periphery of Chicago).
- Power is all, or almost all. As Link and Phelan, Aggleton and Parker and Jacquet affirm, people cannot be shamed and/or blamed in its absence. Hence, the groups selected for reference in this short

text. But it is indubitably the case that quite other groups—like the investment bankers who delivered the global financial crash of 2008–2009 and the politicians whose deregulatory regimes opened the requisite doors for them and who subsequently opted for austerity as the solution—remain prime candidates for shaming and, more to the point, blaming, *except that there are currently no powerholders in place to level and make the charges stick.*

- Shaming and blaming can and do find routine if *latent* expression in what Kelleher and I (2006) have called the 'enabling sector' of civil society, comprising those informal, discursive community meeting or 'third places' like churches, cafes or bars that can in optimally propitious circumstances translate into influence via the 'protest sector' of civil society and the public sphere of the lifeworld (Oldenberg, 1989; Tjora & Scambler, 2013). Financiers, rentiers, CEOs and their ilk are noisily castigated for all that their multiple and *ubiquitous* castigators are compelled by their political impotence to fume and wait in the wings of the lifeworld. It is one thing to revile, another to launch destructive broadsides.
- As Goffman intimates and Durkheim convincingly theorises, shaming and blaming feature in and are functional for *all* social formations: normality is not possible in the absence of abnormality, and this more or less binary distinction *must be* and invariably *is* institutionalised one way or another (Scambler, 2009). Given that power just as invariably intrudes into, and typically decisively at that, prevailing cultural norms, the latter are ripe for sociological interrogation.
- In Britain, as only too frequently elsewhere, prevailing norms 'dictating' attributions of shame and blame are contestable.
- 'Contestation' calls for, *requires*, a sociological engagement beyond Burawoy's (2005) four sociologies, beyond even his favoured public sociology, embracing what I have termed 'foresight' and 'action sociologies' (Scambler, 2018a). In other words, sociology cannot and must not submit to, be tamed by, the institutional artifices of increasingly neoliberal power-holding and power-holders. It *must* embrace both 'alternative futures' (foresight sociology) and contest, above all else, class/command, oligarchic dominance (action sociology).

But how are forms of shaming and blaming that issue from structural relations or mechanisms of power to be resisted? And how might sociology, most conspicuously via foresight and action sociology, contribute?

Resisting Shaming and Blaming

It should be remembered that cultural norms governing attributions of shame and blame come in all shapes and sizes, and if none are entirely divorced from the possession and use of power, their structural origins can be elusive. Moreover, shaming and blaming can on occasion survive rational deliberation and scrutiny—child sex abuse and incidents of what has come to be called 'hate crime', for example—so the scope for resistance is necessarily circumscribed. In this concluding section, the focus will be on exposing and tracing macro- to micro-linkages.

It has been contended throughout that neoliberalism is the ideology that delivers the principal narrative for, and ultimately rationalises, the present era of financial capitalism. Consonant with this, Fraser (2019) has argued that the twenty-first century has witnessed new forms of populism manifest in the election of Trump in the USA and Brexit in the UK. Her analysis offers a nuanced frame for a reconsideration of the family of concepts that include 'the stranger' or 'outcast', 'othering', 'exclusion', 'stigmatisation' and so on.

Calling on Gramsci, she contends that what made Trump and Brexit possible was the breakup of a previous 'hegemonic bloc' and the discrediting of its distinctive normative nexus of distribution and recognition. She refers to this increasingly defunct hegemonic bloc as *progressive neoliberalism*. This comprised two unlikely elements: 'on the one hand, liberal currents emanating from the new social movements (feminism, antiracism, multiculturalism, environmentalism and LGBTQ+rights); on the other hand, the most dynamic, high-end, 'symbolic', and financial sectors of the US economy (Wall Street, Silicon Valley, and Hollywood)' (Fraser, 2019: 11). The cement that held these elements together was a particular combination of views on distribution and recognition, namely an expropriative, plutocratic economic programme with a liberal-meritocratic politics of recognition.

The demise of the hegemonic bloc of progressive neoliberalism has been succeeded by an interregnum. Fraser sees little evidence of either a revised version of progressive neoliberalism or 'a trumped-up hyper-reactionary neoliberalism' emerging in the form of a new hegemonic politics. Hence, the title of her book, a quotation from Gramsci: *the old is dying and the new cannot be born*. So how does she interpret the present, unstable phase of financial capitalism? And are there candidates for a new 'counterhegemonic bloc'? Fraser asks if some form of populism might provide a candidate.

She sees some common ground between supporters of Sanders and Trump in the USA and Remainers and Brexiteers in the UK, namely their rejection of the neoliberal politics of distribution in 2015–2016. Whether these 'masses' can be welded together in a new counterhegemonic bloc is another matter. For that to happen the working-class supporters of Sanders and Trump, of Remainers and Brexiteers, would have to see themselves as allies against an economy rigged to their detriment and in need of transformation. What she calls *reactionary populism* has little prospect of delivering such an alliance. Its hierarchical and exclusionary politics of recognition would seem to preclude it, not least because major sectors of the American and British working and middle classes include many women, members of ethnic minorities, migrants and so on. Fraser goes on to conclude that *progressive populism* is the most likely candidate for a new counterhegemonic bloc: *progressive populism holds out the prospect of egalitarian redistribution with nonhierarchical recognition*. She expands on this in the following words:

> renouncing the progressive-neoliberal stress on personal attitudes, (a progressive-populist bloc) must focus its efforts on the structural-institutional bases of contemporary society. Especially important, it must highlight the shared roots of class and status injustices in financialised capitalism. Conceiving of that system as a single, integrated social totality, it must link the harms suffered by women, immigrants, people of colour, and LGBTQ+people to those experienced by the working-class strata now drawn to right-wing populism. In that way it can lay the foundation for a powerful new coalition among all those now being betrayed by Trump and his counterparts – not just immigrants, feminists, and people of colour who already oppose his hyper-reactionary neoliberalism, but also the white working-class strata who have so far supported it. (Fraser, 2019: 35–36)

Fraser's analysis is consonant with my thesis, outlined in more detail elsewhere (Scambler, 2018a, 2018b). Effective resistance to attributions of shame and blame is reliant, in the last resort, on structural, cultural and institutional change, and key to such change is class mobilisation. Fraser's emphasis on the pairing of redistribution and recognition is an eloquent and welcome elaboration of this thesis.

It does not of course follow from this that we must await a root-and-branch, 'revolutionary' societal transformation. Several comments are in order here. The first is that just as there are many and different dimensions or aspects to vulnerability, so there are to stigma and deviance. It has proved possible to more or less successfully contest some shaming and/or blaming (e.g. in relation to gay rights), but not others (e.g. in relation to refugee rights): most resistance is probably best summarised as work in progress. Second, and to pick up on Fraser's macro-perspective, programmes to counter widespread stigmatisation that rely on changing attitudes: (a) almost invariably entail change 'in the slow lane', and (b) are likely to fall foul of the well-known 'words and deeds' fallacy (i.e. people articulate changes of attitude that when the circumstances arise only too rarely translate into changes of behaviour). (a) and (b) are perhaps best illustrated by the largely American research on mental illness and stigma reduction (Scambler, 2009). Third, what was earlier characterised as 'project stigma' and 'project deviance'—that is, individuals' determination not to remain passive receptors or 'victims' of enacted stigma and/or deviance, or indeed of felt stigma and/or deviance—should be more fully recognised as a force for change.

A final remark concerns what I have called 'permanent reform' (Scambler, 2018a, 2018b). This concept denotes a strategy for inducing change that acknowledges the existence of both a plethora of objections and mobilisations against the status quo and the absence of any ready consensus on 'what next'. (There is in fact something approaching agreement amongst sociologists that financial capitalism is likely to implode and self-destruct by mid-century *and* that 'alternate futures' are uncertain and unpredictable (Wallerstein et al., 2013)). Permanent reform entails a commitment to the building of alliances towards what Fraser calls progressive populism via a series of 'winnable' campaigns that: (a) challenge the neoliberal status quo, and (b) expose its structural infrastructure, most significantly its germination in relations of class and class struggle.

This might seem a long way from Goffman's dramaturgy. Elias taught us that historical processes often unfold slowly and that individual and group dynamics are more often than not caught up in, and are only fully explicable in terms of, these processes. I have sought in this contribution to begin to make good a deficit in macro- and, to a lesser degree, meso-sociological inputs into the sociology of shaming and blaming, most significantly by highlighting the role of power and by referring to the wilful and carefully calculated weaponising of stigma towards the politically expedient category of abjection. The abject can most easily be sanctioned, punished and abandoned by the state.

References

Bourdieu, P. (1980). *The logic of practice*. Cambridge: Polity Press.
Burawoy, M. (2005). For public sociology. *American Sociological Review, 70*, 4–28.
Durkheim, E. (1897). *Suicide* (p. 1952). London: Routledge & Kegan Paul.
Fraser, N. (2019). *The old is dying and the new cannot be born*. London: Verso.
Hopkins, A. (1987). The causes and precipitation of seizures. In A. Hopkins (Ed.), *Epilepsy*. London: Chapman Hall.
Jacquet, J. (2015). *Is shame necessary? New uses for an old tool*. London: Allen Lane.
Link, B., & Phelan, J. (2001). Conceptualising stigma. *Annual Review of Sociology, 27*, 363–385.
Mills, C. W. (1956). *The power elite*. New York: Oxford University Press.
Oldenburg, R. (1989). *The great good third place*. New York: Da Capo Press.
Parker, R., & Aggleton, P. (2003). HIV and AIDS-related stigma and discrimination: A conceptual framework and implications for action. *Social Science and Medicine, 57*, 13–24.
Scambler, G. (2009). Review article: Health-related stigma. *Sociology of Health and Illness, 31*, 441–455.
Scambler, G. (2018a). *Sociology, health and the fractured society: A critical realist account*. London: Routledge.
Scambler, G. (2018b). Heaping blame on shame: 'Weaponising stigma' for neoliberal times. *Sociological Review, 66*, 766–782.
Scambler, G. (2018c). Dimensions of vulnerability salient for health: A sociological approach. *Society, Health and Vulnerability, 10*, 1–26.
Scambler, G., & Kelleher, D. (2006). New social and health movements: Issues of representation and change. *Critical Public Health, 16*, 219–231.
Scambler, G., Afentouli, P., & Selai, C. (2010). Discerning biological, psychological and social mechanisms in the impact of epilepsy on the individual. In G. Scambler & S. Scambler (Eds.), *New directions in the sociology of chronic and disabling conditions: Assaults on the lifeworld*. London: Palgrave Macmillan.
Tjora, A., & Scambler, G. (Eds.). (2013). *Café society*. New York: Palgrave Macmillan.
Tyler, I. (2013). *Revolting subjects: Social abjection and resistance in neoliberal Britain*. London: Zed Books.
Wacquant, L. (2008). *Urban outcasts: A comparative sociology of advanced marginality*. Cambridge: Polity Press.
Wallerstein, I., Collins, R., Mann, M., Derluguian, G., & Calhoun, C. (2013). *Does capitalism have a future?* Oxford: Oxford University Press.

CHAPTER 7

Conclusion

Abstract In a short conclusion, it is argued that sociology's contribution to understanding norms of shame and blame is a crucial one. Reference is made to foresight and action sociologies here. A commitment to the development of these two forms of sociology is commended in the context of contemporary and topical debate.

Keywords Foresight sociology · Action sociology · Permanent reform

While I was writing this book, a video emerged of a 15-year-old boy being grabbed by the neck, thrown to the floor and having water poured over his face at a school in Huddersfield. The boy was Syrian and representative of a number of Syrian refugees forced to flee their country in the wake of the civil war that broke out in 2011. This civil war has devastated much of Syria and forced upwards of 5.6 million people to flee. In 2019, it is still unsafe and people are reluctant to return. In 2015, UK Prime Minister Cameron undertook to resettle 20,000 Syrian refugees in the UK over a five-year period. The 15-year-old who was assaulted left Homs with his family in 2010 and lived in Lebanon until the family was brought to Britain in 2017. The headlines his assault at school made prompted assertions, for example from Refugee Action UK, that this incident was far from exceptional. A report in the Independent newspaper linked a sharp increase in abuse and hate crimes against refugees—and extending to many other examples of racism and sexism (as well as the likes of ageism and disablism)—to the EU referendum and Brexit (Hall, Agerholm, & Dearden, 2018).

Notwithstanding the likely causal salience of biological and psychological mechanisms for any explanation of the behaviour of this Syrian boy's assailant, it should by now be apparent that social mechanisms too are critical constituents of a comprehensive explanatory account. Sociology's is a vital if contributory perspective in society as an open system. But the lifeworld of the young Syrian is not detached: it is permeated and often colonised by system imperatives. Lifeworld and system always each supply pieces to a complex jigsaw. Nor is this just a matter of factoring in the divisions made manifest in the UK by the obdurate haggling over Brexit. Brexit might well have released and boosted forces of hyper-reactionary populism, but this cultural shift has its roots in geopolitics and the enduring structures or relations of class, gender, race, ethnicity and so on that inform it.

In a similar vein, the increasing incidence of hate crimes directed at people with long-term sicknesses or disabilities is part and parcel of a politics of austerity that can only be properly grasped sociologically with reference to the revised class/command dynamic of financial capitalism. The homeless too are a symptom of this same dynamic. More circuitously, migrants and sex workers are often by-products of the global reach of an increasingly transnational capitalist class via the 'push' of war and the feminisation of poverty, respectively (though it is important, as should be clear from the study of 'opportunist sex workers' cited earlier, never to deny people their agency). The principal goal of this book will have been accomplished if this has been conveyed. It is a message which commends a programme of research that aspires to travel well beyond the territory mapped so clearly by Goffman. Elements of a theoretically progressive body of research for the future might accent:

- intersectional enquiries into system imperatives critical for shaming and blaming emanating from structures or relations like class, gender and race or ethnicity;
- the role of middle-range theories that aid our understanding of how macro-phenomena translate into, and to varying extents across, figurations or contexts of shaming and blaming;
- specific case studies of shaming and blaming that trace their system-to-lifeworld or macro- through meso- to micro-explanatory pathways;

- highly focused interdisciplinary initiatives that throw light on the relevance and interplay of, in particular, psychological and social mechanisms for shaming and blaming;
- further exploration of the potential of metareflection—namely, the revisiting of extant theory and empirical research—for illuminating shaming and blaming and heralding a more comprehensive sociology of shaming and blaming.

I conclude by referring back to Habermas on morals and ethics (see Chapter 2). It will be recalled that he rooted his approach to morals in the principle of universalisation. This asserts that for a norm to be valid it must meet the following conditions: *all* those affected can accept the consequences and by-products that its *general* observance can be anticipated to have for the satisfaction of *everyone's* interests. It is a principle that revolves around the questions of justice and solidarity. Ethics, on the other hand, has to do with the 'good life', an issue that can only be broached in relation to particular substantive cultures, ways of life or individual projects. Habermas went on to emphasise the significance of his analysis of discourse ethics for legal systems in general and for deliberative democracy in particular. How is his line of reasoning relevant here?

Drawing on Habermas' formal or procedural analysis, it is, I submit, logically possible—if of course empirically challenging—to ground a rational and consensual 'wheat-from-the-chaff' reappraisal of existing power-based social norms pertaining to shame and blame. This would not, nor should it, do away with shame and blame; but it would allow for and promote a deliberative and democratic reassessment and subsequent commitment to revision, pragmatically via a strategy of permanent reform. This would necessarily announce an affinity with my understanding of the sociological project (Scambler, 1996). To refer once more to the potential for developing foresight and action sociologies, immediate challenges for sociologists would/should include experimenting with alternative—rational, consensual—modes of social organisation, and active, politically engaged resistance to power-holders' strategic underwriting *only* of norms conducive to their material interests.

REFERENCES

Hall, R., Agerholm, H., & Dearden, L. (2018, November 29). Attack on Syrian schoolboy exposes 'toxic environment' faced by refugees in the UK.

Scambler, G. (1996). The 'project of modernity' and the parameters for a critical sociology: An argument with illustrations from medical sociology. *Sociology, 30*, 567–581.

References

Agathangelou, A. (2004). *The global political economy of sex: Desire, violence and insecurity in Mediterranean nation states*. London: Palgrave.
Agustin, L. (2006). The conundrum of women's agency: Migration and the sex industry. In R. Campbell & M. O'Neill (Eds.), *Sex work now* (pp. 116–140). Cullompton: Willan Press.
Amin, A. (2012). *Land of strangers*. Cambridge: Polity Press.
Archer, M. (2007a). The trajectory of the morphogenetic approach: An account in the first person. *Sociologica, Problemas e Practicus, 54,* 35–347.
Archer, M. (2007b). *Making our way in the world*. Cambridge: Cambridge University Press.
Archer, M. (2012). *The reflexive imperative*. Cambridge: Cambridge University Press.
Archer, M. (2014). The generative mechanisms re-configuring late modernity. In M. Archer (Ed.), *Late modernity* (pp. 92–118). New York: Springer.
Ashley, J. (1973). *Journey into silence*. Oxford: Bodley Head.
Barnard, M. (1993). Violence and vulnerability: Conditions of work for streetworking prostitutes. *Sociology of Health and Illness, 15,* 683–705.
Bauman, Z. (1998). On postmodern uses of sex. *Theory, Culture and Society, 15,* 19–33.
Beaumont, P. (2018, June 19). Record 68.5 million people feeling war or persecution worldwide. *The Guardian*.
Bhaskar, R. (2016). *Enlightened common sense: The philosophy of critical realism*. London: Routledge.
Bourdieu, P. (1980). *The logic of practice*. Cambridge: Polity Press.
Bourdieu, P. (1996). *Photography*. Cambridge: Polity Press.

Brewis, J., & Linstead, S. (1998). Time after time: The temporal organisation of red-collar work. *Time and Society, 7*, 223–248.
Brock, T., Carrigan, M., & Scambler, G. (2017). Introduction. In T. Brock, M. Carrigan, & G. Scambler (Eds.), *Structure, culture and agency: Selected papers of Margaret Archer*. London: Routledge.
Bukodi, E., & Goldthorpe, J. (2019). *Social mobility and education in Britain*. Cambridge: Cambridge University Press.
Burawoy, M. (2005). For public sociology. *American Sociological Review, 70*, 4–28.
Carroll, W. (2008). The corporate elite and the transformation of financial capital. In M. Savage & K. Williams (Eds.), *Remembering elites* (pp. 49–62). Oxford: Blackwell.
Castells, M. (2019). *Rupture: The crisis of liberal democracy*. Cambridge: Polity Press.
Clark, T., & Heath, A. (2014). *Hard times: The divisive toll of the economic slump*. New Haven, CT: Yale University Press.
Clement, W., & Myles, J. (1997). *Relations of ruling: Class and gender in postindustrial societies*. Toronto: McGill Queen's University Press.
Cronin, C., & De Greiff, P. (1998). Introduction. In J. Habermas, *The inclusion of the other: Studies in political theory*. Cambridge: Polity Press.
Davis, A. (2018). *Reckless opportunists: Elites at the end of the establishment*. Manchester: Manchester University Press.
Dawe, A. (1970). The two sociologies. *British Journal of Sociology, 21*, 207–218.
Day, S., & Ward, H. (2004). Approaching health through the prism of stigma: Research in seven European countries. In S. Day & H. Ward (Eds.), *Sex work, mobility and health in Europe* (pp. 139–159). London: Routledge & Kegan Paul.
Deleuze, G., & Guattari, F. (1987). *A thousand plateaus: Capitalism and schizophrenia*. Minneapolis: University of Minneapolis Press.
Durkheim, E. (1897). *Suicide* (p. 1952). London: Routledge & Kegan Paul.
Durkheim, E. (1982). *The rules of sociological method*. New York: Free Press.
Elias, N. (2000). *The civilising process: Sociogenetic and psychogenetic investigations*. Oxford: Blackwell.
Elias, N., & Scotson, J. (2008). *The established and the outsiders*. Dublin: University of Dublin Press.
Fraser, N. (2019). *The old is dying and the new cannot be born*. London: Verso.
Garthwaite, K. (2016). *Hunger pains: Life inside foodbank Britain*. Bristol: Policy Press.
Giddens, A. (1992). *The transformation of intimacy: Sexuality, love and eroticism*. Cambridge: Polity Press.
Goffman, E. (1968a). *Stigma: The management of spoiled identity*. Harmondsworth: Penguin.

Goffman, E. (1968b). *Asylums: Essays on the social situation of mental patients and other inmates.* Harmondsworth: Penguin.

Goffman, E. (1969). *The presentation of self in everyday life.* Harmondsworth: Penguin.

Goffman, E. (1971). *Relations in public: Microstudies of the social order.* New York: Basic Books.

Greenfield, P., & Marsh, S. (2018). Deaths of UK homeless people more than double in five years. *The Guardian.* www.theguardian.com//society/2018/apr/11/deaths-of-uk-homeless-people-more-than-double-in-five-years.

Gross, N. (2005). The de-traditionalisation of intimacy reconsidered. *Sociological Theory, 23,* 286–311.

Habermas, J. (1975). *Legitimation crisis.* London: Heinemann.

Habermas, J. (1984). *Theory of communicative action, volume 1: Reason and the rationalization of society.* London: Heinemann.

Habermas, J. (1987). *Theory of communicative action, volume 2: Lifeworld and system: A critique of functionalist reason.* Cambridge: Polity Press.

Habermas, J. (1989). *The new conservatism.* Cambridge: Cambridge University Press.

Habermas, J. (1990). *Moral consciousness and communicative action.* Cambridge: Polity Press.

Habermas, J. (1993). *Justification and application: Remarks on discourse ethics.* Cambridge: Polity Press.

Habermas, J. (1996). *Between facts and norms: Contributions to discourse theory of law and democracy.* Cambridge: Polity Press.

Hall, R., Agerholm, H., & Dearden, L. (2018, November 29). Attack on Syrian schoolboy exposes 'toxic environment' faced by refugees in the UK.

Homeless.org.uk. (2018). www.homeless.org.uk/facts/homelessness-in-numbers/rough-sleeping-our-analysis.

Hopkins, A. (1987). The causes and precipitation of seizures. In A. Hopkins (Ed.), *Epilepsy.* London: Chapman Hall.

Independent. (2019). More than 100 women in Yarl's Wood detention centre go on hunger strike over 'inhumane' conditions. https://www.independent.co.uk/home-news/yarls-wood-women…ration-detention-centre-hunger-strike-home-office-a8223886.html. Accessed 14 March 2019.

International Organisation for Migration (IOM). (2011). *Glossary on migration.* http://migrationdataportal.org/themes/forced-migration-or-displacement/. Accessed 16 May 2018.

Jacquet, J. (2015). *Is shame necessary? New uses for an old tool.* London: Allen Lane.

Landes, D. (1998). *Wealth and poverty of nations.* London: Little, Brown & Co.

Link, B., & Phelan, J. (2001). Conceptualising stigma. *Annual Review of Sociology, 27,* 363–385.

Lyotard, J.-F. (1984). *The postmodern condition*. Manchester: Manchester University Press.
McIntyre, N., & Rice-Oxley, M. (2018, June 20). The list—It's 34,361 and rising: How the list tallies Europe's migrant bodycount. *The Guardian*.
McKenzie, L. (2015). *Getting by: Estates, class and culture*. Bristol: Policy Press.
McKenzie, L. (2017). Valuing and strengthening community. In R. Atkinson, L. McKenzie, & S. Winlow (Eds.), *Building better societies: Promoting social justice in a world falling apart*. Bristol: Policy Press.
Merton, T. (1968). *Social theory and social structure*. New York: Free Press.
Mills, C. W. (1956). *The power elite*. New York: Oxford University Press.
Observer Editorial. (2019). The Observer view on Britain failing dismally in its moral duty to help refugees. https://www.theguardian.com/commentisfree/2019/jan/06/observer-view-on-britain-failing-in-moral-duty-to-help-refugees. Accessed 14 March 2019.
O'Connell Davidson, J. (1998). *Prostitution, power and freedom*. Cambridge: Polity Press.
Oldenburg, R. (1989). *The great good third place*. New York: Da Capo Press.
Papworth Trust. (2013). *Disability in the United Kingdom 2013: Facts and figures*. http://www.papworth.org.uk. Accessed 6 August 2017.
Parker, R., & Aggleton, P. (2003). HIV and AIDS-related stigma and discrimination: A conceptual framework and implications for action. *Social Science and Medicine, 57*, 13–24.
Parsons, T. (1951). *The social system*. London: Routledge.
Petintseva, O. (2015). Approaching new migration through Elias' 'established' and 'outsider' lens. https://lib.umich.edu/h/humfig/11217607.0004.304/--approaching-new--migration-through-eliass-established?rgn=main;view=fulltext. Accessed 4 October 2018.
Pheterson, G. (1993). The whore stigma: Female dishonour and male unworthiness. *Social Text, 37*, 39–54.
Piketty, T. (2014). *Capital in the twenty-first century*. Cambridge, MA: Harvard University Press.
Quintaneiro, T. (2004). The concept of figuration or configuration in Norbert Elias' sociological theory. *Teoria & Sociedade, 12*, 54–69.
Refugee Council. (2019). *Top 20 facts about refugees and people seeking asylum*. https://www.refugeecouncil.org.uk/topfacts. Accessed 12 March 2019.
Ringdal, N. (2004). *Love for sale: A global history of prostitution*. London: Atlantic Books.
Sanders, T. (2005). 'It's just acting': Sex workers' strategies for capitalising on sexuality. *Gender, Work and Organisation, 12*, 319–342.
Scambler, G. (1987). Habermas and the power of medical expertise. In G. Scambler (Ed.), *Sociological theory and medical sociology* (pp. 165–193). London: Tavistock.

Scambler, G. (1989). *Epilepsy*. London: Tavistock.
Scambler, G. (1996). The 'project of modernity' and the parameters for a critical sociology: An argument with illustrations from medical sociology. *Sociology, 30*, 567–581.
Scambler, G. (Ed.). (2001). *Habermas, critical theory and health*. London: Routledge.
Scambler, G. (2007). Sex work stigma: Opportunist migrants in London. *Sociology, 41*, 1079–1096.
Scambler, G. (2009a). Review article: Health-related stigma. *Sociology of Health and Illness, 31*, 441–455.
Scambler, G. (2009b). Stigma and mental illness. In D. Pilgrim, A. Rogers, & B. Pescosolido (Eds.), *The sage handbook of mental health and illness*. London: Sage.
Scambler, G. (2012). Archer, morphogenesis and the role of agency in the sociology of health inequalities. In G. Scambler (Ed.), *Contemporary theorists for medical sociology* (pp. 131–149). London: Routledge.
Scambler, G. (2018a). *Sociology, health and the fractured society: A critical realist account*. London: Routledge.
Scambler, G. (2018b). Heaping blame on shame: 'Weaponising stigma' for neoliberal times. *Sociological Review, 66*, 766–782.
Scambler, G. (2018c). Dimensions of vulnerability salient for health: A sociological approach. *Society, Health and Vulnerability, 10*, 1–26.
Scambler, G., & Hopkins, A. (1986). 'Being epileptic': Coming to terms with stigma. *Sociology of Health and Illness, 8*, 26–43.
Scambler, G., & Kelleher, D. (2006). New social and health movements: Issues of representation and change. *Critical Public Health, 16*, 219–231.
Scambler, G., & Paoli, F. (2008). Health work, female sex workers and HIV/AIDS: Global and local dimensions of stigma and deviance as barriers to effective interventions. *Social Science and Medicine, 65*, 1–15.
Scambler, G., & Scambler, S. (2015). Theorising health inequalities: The untapped potential of dialectical critical realism. *Social Theory and Health, 13*, 340–354.
Scambler, G., Afentouli, P., & Selai, C. (2010). Discerning biological, psychological and social mechanisms in the impact of epilepsy on the individual. In G. Scambler & S. Scambler (Eds.), *New directions in the sociology of chronic and disabling conditions: Assaults on the lifeworld*. London: Palgrave Macmillan.
Sklair, L. (2000). *The transnational capitalist class*. Oxford: Blackwell.
Slater, T. (2014). The myth of 'Broken Britain': Welfare reform and the production of ignorance. *Antipode, 46*, 948–969.
Slater, T. (2018). The invention of the 'sink estate': Consequential categorisation and the UK housing crisis. *Sociological Review, 66*, 877–897.
Smith, D. (2001). *Norbert Elias and modern social theory*. London: Sage.

REFERENCES

Stanley, L. (2017). *Whites writing whiteness.* http://www.whiteswritingwhiteness.ed.ac.uk/thinking-with-elias/the-established-outsider-figuration-race-and-whiteness/. Accessed 4 October 2018.

Streeck, W. (2016). *How will capitalism end?* London: Verso.

Thomas, C. (2007). *Sociologies of illness and disability: Contested ideas in disability studies and medical sociology.* Basingstoke: Palgrave Macmillan.

Thomas, C. (2012). Theorizing disability and chronic illness: Where next for perspectives in medical sociology? *Social Theory and Health, 10,* 209–228.

Tjora, A., & Scambler, G. (Eds.). (2013). *Café society.* New York: Palgrave Macmillan.

Tyler, I. (2013). *Revolting subjects: Social abjection and resistance in neoliberal Britain.* London: Zed Books.

Tyler, I. (2018). Resituating Erving Goffman: From stigma power to black power. *Sociological Review, 66,* 744–765.

Wacquant, L. (2008). *Urban outcasts: A comparative sociology of advanced marginality.* Cambridge: Polity Press.

Wallerstein, I., Collins, R., Mann, M., Derluguian, G., & Calhoun, C. (2013). *Does capitalism have a future?* Oxford: Oxford University Press.

Warr, D., Taylor, G., & Williams, R. (2017). Artfully thinking the prosocial. In R. Atkinson, L. Mckenzie, & S. Winlow (Eds.), *Building better societies: Promoting social justice in a world falling apart.* Bristol: Policy Press.

Wittgenstein, L. (1958). *Philosophical investigations* (2nd ed.). Oxford: Blackwell.

Index

A
Abjects, 80, 98
Activity reinforcement, 48, 56
Agathangelou, A., 58
Agency, 2, 3, 10–12, 20, 23, 37, 40–44, 48, 49, 51, 52, 54–57, 59, 106
Agerholm, H., 106
Aggleton, P., 93, 94, 98
Agustin, L., 51
Amin, A., 77–79
Archer, M., 11, 40, 42, 43, 48, 49
  transitory autonomous reflexives, 54, 56
  types of reflexivity, 48, 49
Ashley, J., 2, 6
Asylum seekers, 3–5, 73, 74, 76
ATOS, 72, 73
Austerity, 5, 35, 37, 39, 43, 69, 72, 95, 99, 106

B
Barnard, M., 53
Bauman, Z., 58

Beaumont, P., 5
Bhaskar, R.
  demi-regularities, 22
  epistemic fallacy, 21
  experience, events, real, 21
  open systems, 21
Biological mechanisms, 89
Bourdieu, P., 40–43, 89–91, 96, 98
Brewis, J., 53
Brexit, 4, 5, 68, 70, 71, 73, 78, 84, 96, 100, 106
Brock, T., 42
Bukodi, E., 63, 65

C
Capitalism
  financial capitalism, 12, 24, 27, 33, 36, 43, 50, 57, 61–63, 67, 68, 71, 72, 78, 79, 90, 92, 97, 98, 100, 102, 106
  liberal capitalism, 62
  welfare capitalism, 62
Capital monopolists, 66–68, 94
Carrigan, M., 42

Carroll, W., 63
Castells, M., 69, 70
Clark, T., 68
Class/command dynamic, 63, 67, 71, 72, 77–79, 92, 96, 106
Class relations, 57, 58, 97
　objective class, 71
　subjective class, 71
Clement, W., 63
Command relations, 58, 70, 77, 97
Critical realism, 11, 12, 21–23, 27, 40, 42, 63, 88
Critical theory, 11, 21, 23, 40
Cronin, C., 32
Cultural facilitation, 56
Culture, 2, 3, 6, 11, 23, 30, 32, 40–44, 51, 54, 56, 58, 59, 68, 70, 87, 93, 98, 107

D
Dark money, 80, 83
Davis, A., 67
Dawe, A., 20
Day, S., 59
Dearden, L., 106
De Greiff, P., 32
Deleuze, G., 53
Deviance
　enacted, 26, 39, 50, 53, 55, 92, 98, 102
　felt, 26, 35, 39, 50, 53, 55, 59, 92, 102
　project, 26, 40, 55, 102
Disability theory
　disability politics, 6, 71
　oppression paradigm, 72
　personal tragedy paradigm, 71
Disabled, 6–8, 18, 22, 26, 33, 71, 72, 79, 88, 98
Durkheim, E., 1, 18, 90, 99

E
Ego adjustment, 48, 56
Elias, N., 18–23, 102
Employment and Support Allowance (ESA), 72, 73
Epilepsy, 26, 27
　epilepsy related quality of life (ERQOL), 88, 89
Established-outsiders dichotomy, 21
Ethnic/race relations, 58, 77, 79, 80, 91, 96, 97, 106
European Union (EU), 4, 5, 22, 69, 70, 73, 74, 78, 106

F
Feminisation of poverty, 58, 106
Fictional case study, 95
Foodbanks, 33–36, 38, 39, 44, 72, 84, 96

G
Garthwaite, K., 33–36, 38, 39
Gender relations, 58, 59, 96
Giddens, A., 57
Global financial crisis, 63, 69
Goffman, E.
　discreditable identity, 17, 92
　discredited identity, 17
　dramaturgical analysis, 16, 18, 19, 34, 39
　Goffman's limitations, 18, 24, 34
　types of stigma, 17
Goldthorpe, J., 63, 65
Governing oligarchy, 22, 67
Greenfield, P., 9
Gross, N., 58
Guattari, F., 53

H

Habermas, J.
  communicative and strategic action, 24, 25, 30, 34
  discourse ethics, 30, 32, 107
  ideal speech situation, 24, 30
  legitimation crisis, 62
  lifeworld, 3, 11, 23–25, 29, 30, 34, 54, 67, 81, 94, 97
  system, 11, 23–25, 30, 54, 97
  system colonisation, 25, 67, 94, 97
Hall, R., 105
Heath, A., 68
Higher immorality, 68
Homeless, 3, 8, 18, 22, 26, 33, 35, 88, 98, 106
  rough sleepers, 9
Hopkins, A., 88

I

Identity formation, 67
Inequality, 57, 68

J

Jacquet, J., 94, 98

L

Landes, D., 67
Link, B., 93, 94, 98
Linstead, S., 53
Long-term sick, 3, 6, 18, 22, 26, 33
Lyotard, J.F., 57

M

Marsh, S., 9
McIntyre, N., 5
McKenzie, L., 36, 37, 39
Mechanisms (causal), 20, 21, 27, 43, 63

Merton, T., 27, 47
Metareflection, 11, 47, 56, 84, 88, 107
Migrants, 3–5, 9, 10, 18, 20–22, 25, 26, 33, 49, 51–53, 56, 61, 69, 71, 73, 78, 79, 88, 92, 96, 101, 106
Mills, C.W., 68, 91
Moral deficit, 2, 26, 79, 98
Myles, J., 63

N

Neoliberal ideology, 67, 68, 84

O

O'Connell Davidson, J., 53
Oldenburg, R., 99
Ontological deficit, 2, 26, 79, 98

P

Papworth Trust, 8
Parker, R., 93, 94, 98
Parsons, T., 47
Permanent reform, 102, 107
Personal Independence Payments (PIP), 73
Petintseva, O., 19, 20
Phelan, J., 93, 94, 98
Pheterson, G., 50, 51, 53
Piketty, T., 67
Populism, 100, 106
  progressive populism, 101, 102
  reactionary populism, 101
Power, 4, 16, 19, 20, 22–25, 32, 33, 41, 43, 57, 63, 67, 76, 80, 88, 90–95, 97–100, 102
  power elite, 67, 77, 83, 98
Psychological mechanisms, 23, 44, 88, 89, 94, 106

Q

Quintaneiro, T., 19

R

Refugee Council, 73, 77
Refugees, 3–5, 9, 18–22, 25, 26, 33, 61, 71, 73–79, 88, 91, 98, 102, 105
Resistance, 26, 40, 50, 80, 90, 100–102, 107
Rice-Oxley, M., 5
Ringdal, N., 58

S

Sanders, T., 53, 101
Scambler, G., 3, 8, 10, 21, 23, 24, 26, 30, 32, 38, 40, 42, 48, 50, 51, 53, 56, 57, 59, 62, 63, 66–68, 73, 80, 89, 90, 93, 95, 97, 99, 101, 102, 107
Scotson, J., 19
Sex workers
  hierarchy, 10, 50, 92
  opportunist migrants, 48, 54, 57, 58
  types, 50
Sink estate, 36, 44, 83
Slater, T., 36, 80, 83
Smith, D., 19
Social integration, 30, 62
Social mechanisms, 12, 54, 88, 89, 94, 106, 107
Stanley, L., 20
Stigma
  enacted, 26, 27, 34, 39, 50, 53, 55, 89, 92, 98, 102
  felt, 26, 27, 34, 35, 39, 50, 53, 55, 59, 89, 92, 102
  project, 26, 27, 40, 55, 102
Strangers, 1, 19, 22, 50, 73, 77–79, 89, 100

Streeck, W., 12
Structure, 2, 6, 11, 15, 16, 18–20, 23, 40–44, 48, 49, 54, 56, 59, 61, 63, 67, 71, 79, 83, 84, 87, 92, 97, 98, 106
Syria, 5, 22, 73, 76, 77, 105
System integration, 30, 62

T

Taylor, G., 39
Territorial stigma, 36, 39, 54, 83
Think tanks, 80, 81, 83
Thomas, C., 6, 71
Tyler, I., 18, 98

U

United Kingdom Independence Party (UKIP), 69

V

Vulnerability, 9, 90–92, 95, 96
  dimensions of vulnerability, 90, 96, 102

W

Wacquant, L., 98
Ward, H., 59
Warr, D., 39, 43
Weaponising of stigma, 27, 79, 84, 92, 96, 102
Williams, R., 39
'Winston Parva', 19
Wittgenstein, L., 1, 15
Work Capability Assessments (WCA), 72

Y

Yarl's Wood, 78

CPI Antony Rowe
Eastbourne, UK
December 04, 2019